# A NOTE-BOOK OF
# EDMUND BURKE

EDMUND BURKE and CHARLES FOX, by Angelica Kauffmann

# A NOTE-BOOK OF EDMUND BURKE

POEMS, CHARACTERS, ESSAYS AND OTHER
SKETCHES IN THE HANDS OF EDMUND AND
WILLIAM BURKE NOW PRINTED FOR THE
FIRST TIME IN THEIR ENTIRETY
AND EDITED

BY

## H. V. F. SOMERSET

CAMBRIDGE
AT THE UNIVERSITY PRESS
1957

CAMBRIDGE UNIVERSITY PRESS
Cambridge, New York, Melbourne, Madrid, Cape Town,
Singapore, São Paulo, Delhi, Tokyo, Mexico City

Cambridge University Press
The Edinburgh Building, Cambridge CB2 8RU, UK

Published in the United States of America by Cambridge University Press, New York

www.cambridge.org
Information on this title: www.cambridge.org/9780521247061

First published 1957
First paperback edition 2011

*A catalogue record for this publication is available from the British Library*

ISBN 978-0-521-24706-1 Paperback

# CONTENTS

# CONTENTS

## PLATES

# ACKNOWLEDGMENTS

I wish to express my appreciation to the Earl Fitzwilliam and his Trustees of the Wentworth Woodhouse Estates for their public spirit in depositing the Burke papers in the Sheffield City Library for the use of students, and for permission to publish the following Note-Book. I have also to express my thanks to the Earl Fitzwilliam for permission to reproduce the portrait of William Burke by Sir Joshua Reynolds, and to the Trustees of the National Gallery of Ireland for allowing me to reproduce the portrait of Edmund Burke with Charles James Fox by Angelica Kauffmann.

I am greatly obliged to Sir Ernest Barker, who with his great knowledge of the period, and with his unfailing generosity, has read my manuscript and advised me on a number of textual points, as well as writing the Foreword. I am also indebted to Mr C. H. Wilkinson and to Mr A. N. Bryan-Brown, both of Worcester College, Oxford, and to Mr John Crow of King's College, London, for sympathetic and useful help on several points. Finally I have to express my appreciation of the meticulous care of the reader at the Cambridge University Press in helping me to revise my proofs, and of the courtesy and helpfulness of the staff of the Sheffield City Library, and especially of Miss Meredith, Librarian of the Department of Local History and Archives.

H. V. F. S.

OXFORD
*November 1956*

# FOREWORD

BY SIR ERNEST BARKER

'To a generous Mind', Burke wrote in a paper he published while he was still an undergraduate at Trinity College, Dublin, 'nothing is so agreeable as to commend the Works of others.' I would not claim generosity for my commendation of this book, but I certainly find it an agreeable office to hang a bush before Mr Somerset's good wine, though I feel that it needs no bush. This Note-Book of Edmund Burke, with the editor's explanatory introduction, throws new light on Burke's thought and the development of his ideas during some six years of his life (from 1750 to 1756) which had hitherto been mainly a blank. Something was already known of his previous years at Trinity College, Dublin: Mr Samuels, in his work on *The Early Life, Correspondence and Writings of Burke*, has told the story of Burke's undergraduate career, and of his busy activity as a journalist and pamphleteer in the thirteen numbers of the *Reformer* and the dozen or so articles which he published in the course of the Lucas controversy (on the rights of Dublin freemen and the powers of the Dublin House of Commons) during the years 1748 and 1749. But we have hitherto known very little of Burke's early years in England, from the spring of 1750, when he came over to England to read for the bar at the Middle Temple, down to the year 1756, when he published his first book on *A Vindication of Natural Society*. The Note-Book which is now published, with its sketches of 'characters' and its general essays, shows the work which he was doing, and the prentice efforts by which he was occupied, during these years, in conjunction with his name-sake and possible kinsman William Burke. Some of the early items in the Note-Book (the

first seven and the ninth) are dated, and the dates run from
1750 to 1754: most of them are without dates, but they are
probably all anterior to the year 1756, after which Burke was
engaged with the composition and publication of a number of
literary works—not only the *Vindication of Natural Society*,
but also the *Essay on the Sublime and Beautiful* of 1757 and the
first volume of the *Annual Register* which appeared in 1758.
Most of the items, and certainly all the important items, are the
work of Edmund Burke (the Editor would assign eighteen of
the twenty-four to his pen, leaving four to William Burke and
two of uncertain authorship); and we may therefore use the
general substance of the Note-Book as evidence of Burke's
thought and the development of his ideas during his early
youth, from the age of 21 (he was 21 when he came to England)
to the age of 27, when he published his first work.

The young Burke, in his views of religion and his ideas of
men and their characters, already anticipates and foreshadows
the mature Burke of later years—the Burke of 1770 and the
*Thoughts on the Cause of the Present Discontents*, and the
Burke of the *Reflections on the Revolution in France* of 1790.
When he writes, in the piece entitled *Religion of No Efficacy
considered as a State Engine* (no. 16), about 'enthusiasm' and
its operation (how it supplies the want of reason, and 'comes
nearer the great and comprehensive Reason in its effects'), he
is already feeling what he felt and expressed long afterwards in
his attack on the metaphysical and geometrical character of
the French Revolution. When, again, he sketches and analyses
'characters', as he does in many of the items of the Note-Book,
he is already giving evidence of that psychological insight,
and that subtle understanding of human motives, which inspired
his later and greater works. It may be, indeed, that he began
by imitating an English trend and tradition of character-
drawing which is already conspicuous in our seventeenth-

century literature (and not least in Clarendon's writings): but if he began as an imitator, he ended as an artist and creator in his own right, and throughout his life he studied and painted characters (characters engaged and moulding action in the great world of politics) as his contemporary Reynolds studied and painted his sitters. One of the loveliest of the characters painted in the Note-Book is that of his wife ('her gravity is a gentle thoughtfulness...her voice is a low soft music'): one of the subtlest is 'the character of a good man', in which he almost seems to be describing himself when he writes that 'his imagination is lively, active, vigorous, quickly taking fire, and generally too powerful for an understanding fitted rather to conspire with it in its excesses than to restrain it'.

On the whole the essays in the Note-Book are the trial flights of a mind that was destined to fly high, and they show Burke finding a style (a noble and distinctive style) and exercising the powers of his thought on the topics which were to engage him for the rest of his life—religion, politics, men's characters and men's motives. They are, in a sense, *juvenilia*; they have, at times, the mannerisms of youth; but they also show a maturity of judgment and an understanding of life. There is shrewdness, and also some sadness, in the essay on 'the way to preferment'; and there is wisdom of a high order in the longest and finest of the essays, on 'philosophy and learning'. Its plea for variety of studies ('that it helps to form that *versatile ingenium* which is of very great use in life') is a plea that is still valid: its defence of the value of conversation and 'discourse', which teaches lessons 'of a better kind than we draw from books', has still its value. Mr Somerset quotes in his introduction a sentence from a later essay, in the *Annual Register* of 1760, which shows Burke's sense of the value of experience and immersion in life's activities, and which attests his eagerness to embark on the full tide of active 'discourse' and debate with his fellows. (It is a sentence which deserves to be remembered and pondered by the academic mind.) 'He that lives in a college, after his mind is sufficiently stocked with learning, is like a man, who having built and rigged a ship, should lock her up in a dry dock.' These essays show Burke building and rigging his ship; but they also show him resolved to sail his ship on the open sea of life.

E.B.

CAMBRIDGE
*July 1956*

To a generous Mind nothing is so agreeable as to commend the Works of others, and to be the Means of ushering into the world such happy Productions, as thro' their prevailing Merit must in Process of Time be esteemed by every Body.

EDMUND BURKE in *The Reformer* (no. 13, 21 April 1748)

Some of the Learned have been very severe upon such works as we now lay before the Public. Their severity would have been just, if such works had been recommended or used to the exclusion of more important studies. Those who aspire to a solid erudition, must undoubtedly take other methods to acquire it. They have their labour and their merit. But there are readers of another order, who must not be left wholly unprovided: For such readers, it is our province to collect matters of a lighter nature; but pleasing even by their levity; by their variety; and their aptitude to enter into common conversation. Things of this sort often gradually and imperceptibly insinuate a taste for knowledge, and in some measure gratify that taste. They steal some moments from the round of dissipation and pleasure. They relieve the minds of men of business,—who cannot pass from severe labour to severe study,—with an elegant relaxation. They preserve the strenuous idleness of many from a worse employment.

EDMUND BURKE, Preface to *The Annual Register* (1758)

# INTRODUCTION

The following poems, characters, essays and other sketches are now printed for the first time, in their entirety, from a note-book preserved among the Burke papers belonging to Earl Fitzwilliam, but now deposited in the Public Library at Sheffield. The note-book measures 8 × 6½ in., and is roughly bound in boards, quarter parchment. It is inscribed 'Found among Mr Wm. Burke's Papers by W. Cuppage'. The contents are partly in the hand of Edmund Burke and partly in that of his 'kinsman' William Burke.

William Burke was known as a kinsman of Edmund's, though their exact relationship has never been made clear.[1] When Edmund first came to London he lodged in the house of William's father; later the two of them continuously resided and travelled together; and, until Edmund's death in 1796, William, when in England, was a member of his household. They were also together involved in many financial trans-actions, in which William played the leading part, and indeed brought no little discredit to his 'cousin' Edmund.[2] But they were also literary collaborators. Nor are William's talents in this field by any means to be despised. Horace Walpole in his *Memoirs of the Reign of King George the Third*[3] tells us, 'William Burke, the cousin of Edmund, wrote with ingenuity and sharpness; and both of them were serviceable to the new Administration (in 1766), by party papers'; and John Almon in his *Biographical, Literary and Political Anecdotes* (1797) has

[1] In fact it was even denied that there was any blood-relationship.
[2] Dixon Wecter, *Burke and his Kinsmen*, University of Colorado Studies, vol. I (1939), *passim*. See also Sir Charles Dilke, *Papers of a Critic* (London, 1875), vol. II, pp. 309–84, and Sir Philip Magnus, *Edmund Burke*.
[3] Edition of 1845, vol. II, pp. 273–4.

a chapter headed 'Messieurs Burkes' in which he discusses Edmund, his brother Richard, his son Richard and William Burke, and writes 'Although it is unquestionably true that the talents of Mr Edmund Burke had infinitely the ascendancy, yet those of Mr Richard Burke, and of Mr William Burke, were greatly above mediocrity', and adds, 'an association of such literary abilities and active minds must undoubtedly have produced many papers, which are now unknown; particularly their occasional Essays, or Letters, in the newspapers; which they were in the habit of furnishing during several years. Many of these are interesting as containing the sense of parties, from the year 1764 or thereabouts';[1] and he tells us of their collaboration in fugitive pieces and in a series of letters signed 'Valens' contributed to the Press, quoting in full 'The Yorkshire Question' by 'Mess^rs Burkes', the 'Management of the London Gazette' by 'Messieurs Burkes', and 'Two Letters on the conduct of Lord Mansfield', by 'Mess^rs. Burkes'.

William Burke is also known to have collaborated with Edmund in the *Account of the European Settlements in America*; and we believe him to have contributed to *The Annual Register*;[2] while in 1759 appeared his pamphlet *Remarks on the Letter to Two Great Men*, and later his *Examination of the Commercial Principles of the Late Negotiation between Great Britain and France in 1761*. Among the Wentworth Woodhouse papers, also, are to be found a number of his essays and papers in manuscript.

Thus we see that William Burke was a writer of some significance; and that the present note-book is far from being the only joint production of 'the Messieurs Burkes'. Meanwhile it would appear that most, if not indeed all, of these pieces were written during the early years of Burke's residence in England. Burke came over from Dublin in 1750. The first dated piece is marked 'Croydon, 1750'.

[1] Almon, *Anecdotes*, vol. II, pp. 345–7.    [2] See below, p. 13.

Since the note-book, however, which contains twenty-four pieces,[1] consists of contributions by William Burke as well as by Edmund, it is important to consider which pieces belong to each, and by what means we are to judge their authorship. We have three tests by which to do this: (i) the written ascriptions in the note-book; (ii) the handwriting; and (iii) the internal evidence of the pieces themselves. But the handwriting is no sure guide. For several pieces definitely indexed, or assigned in writing on the manuscript, to Edmund Burke are either wholly, or in part in the hand of William. Now it would seem likely that those in the handwriting of Edmund were composed by him; while certainly some in the handwriting of William are also Edmund's, since, as we have said, several that are initialled as Edmund's are wholly, or in part, in William's hand. The internal evidence, however, is more important. For some pieces are—as the art critics say of pictures—'signed all over'.

To consider the pieces, then, from these three points of view.

*First,* as regards numbers definitely assigned in writing to one or the other writer, we find that the following are attributed in this way to Edmund Burke:

1   The Muse Divorced.
4   An Answer to the Pillow.
6   An Epistle to Doctor Nugent.
7   A Funeral Oration.
8   A Plan for Arguing.
9   A Letter to Sir James Lowther.
10   The Character of — [Mrs Edmund Burke].
12   Phidippus [William Burke].

---

[1] We have here treated the piece beginning 'Nothing can operate but from its own principles' and the passage beginning 'If there be a God such as we conceive' as two pieces, and have marked them nos. 16 and 17; though in the original index they are treated as one.

while the following are attributed to William Burke:

This accounts for sixteen out of the twenty-four pieces, leaving eight without a written statement of authorship.

*Second,* as regards the handwriting in the remaining eight pieces,[1] nos. 13, 14, 15, 16, 17, 18 and 24 are in William Burke's hand; no. 20 is in Edmund's down to the words 'It is dangerous for a prince to suffer his Capital City to be too extensive', but afterwards in that of William.

*Third,* as regards the internal evidence of these eight un-attributed numbers, which, even if copied out by William Burke, may yet be by Edmund, in no. 13, 'The Way to Prefer-ment', the remarks on the danger of showing one's merit, or superiority, are somewhat similar to certain passages in 'The Character of a Fine Gentleman' (no. 21), which is definitely assigned to Edmund. Moreover, the passage 'I took comfort that my parts, my intrinsic Merit, were a much better posses-sion than his Equipage; tho' I confess... my own Merit made but a poor figure when the said Equipage made its Appear-

---

[1] I.e. 13  The Way to Preferment.
14  The Man of Spirit.
15  A True Genius.
16  Religion...as a State Engine.
17  'If there be a God....'
18  A Dialogue.
20  Some Political...Observations.
24  On Voltaire.

ance', is very reminiscent of a passage in Edmund's 'Epistle to Doctor Nugent':

> And I, who think it is the time's reproach
> To see a Scoundrel Gamester in his Coach,
> Think modestly 'twould have a better Air
> To see my humble self exalted there.

This would lead us to believe that the piece is by Edmund Burke.

No. 14, 'The Man of Spirit', bears a close resemblance to a piece definitely known to be by Edmund. For this study of 'Spirit' provides a close analogy with an essay in Burke's early publication, *The Reformer* (Dublin, 1747), on the error of making 'Spirit', not sense, the essence of good writing;[1] even if the simile at the end, which seems indeed to be a separate piece, is difficult to classify.

No. 15, 'A True Genius', also has something of the stamp of Edmund's outlook and something of his style about it: of his outlook in the rather pained reflection that genius is 'but rarely of any Use; never but on Extraordinary Occasions' and that 'at other times...those are then wanted who lye in an ordinary road'; and of his style in the passage 'A Man who proceeds in the ordinary Method proceeds like a Machine: We know what to oppose to every Motion; we see all his Scheme: We can be sure what Step[s] he will take next, and it is our own fault if he has any success'—the general statement down to 'every Motion', the three short sentences expanding this statement, and then the longer concluding phrase to explain and

---

[1] For no. 12 of Burke's early publication, *The Reformer* (1747–8), see below, p. 12. In it Burke writes, 'There is nothing, on which Men form so various Judgments, and so few just, as on good Writing; but they seem in some measure to have agreed on a kind of Standard which they call *Spirit*. The highest and only Praise they give a Work which they like is "that it is written with Spirit"' (A. P. I. Samuels, *The Early Life, Correspondence and Writings of the Rt. Hon. Edmund Burke* (Cambridge University Press, 1923), p. 324).

illustrate it. This form of rhetoric is common in Burke's writings.

No. 16, 'Religion...', appears on internal evidence to be 'signed all over' in regard both to the thought and the style. The following short sharp sentences, for instance, are particularly typical of Edmund: 'When we are told this, we cool immediately. The springs are seen, we value ourselves on the Discovery, we cast Religion to the Vulgar and lose all restraint....' While the stress on the strength of 'Enthusiasm' as compared with 'Reason' was always a notable feature of Edmund Burke's philosophy[1] and indeed is re-echoed in other of his pieces in the note-book itself.[2]

No. 17, 'If there be a God...', would seem also to be by Edmund, on account of its firm, logical arrangement and of the general character of its argument; for here again appears his typical reliance on feeling rather than on reasoning, where he writes, 'The Arguments against Providence are from our *Reasonings....* There is nothing at all in our natural feelings against it. There is a great deal in our natural feelings for it' (no. 17, p. 71); and again, 'Men do not naturally conceive that, when they are strongly actuated to call upon a Superior... they cannot be heard; they do not conceive that they have Passions which have no Purpose...', and so on, in the same vein; and yet again 'Man has Ideas of Immortality, and wishes for it; he does not think he has Ideas and Wishes, for no end' (no. 17, p. 71). One finds also much of both the strength

---

[1] See Arthur Cobban's study, *Edmund Burke and the Revolt against the Eighteenth Century* (London, 1929).

[2] E.g. in no. 19 (initialled 'E.B.', and written throughout in his handwriting), 'the passions, in which, more than in any faults of reasoning, the Sources of all our Errors lie' (no. 19, p. 88); and in no. 23 (also marked 'E.B.'), 'every passion we have strong enough to make a considerable Principle of Action, is always too strong in some degree for our Reason' (no. 23, p. 118); cf. also in no. 17, 'They naturally measure their Duties to the Divinity by their own wants and their feelings, and not by abstract Speculations. In the one they cannot be deceived, in the other they may' (no. 17).

and the weakness of this piece reflected in Edmund's reported 'Answer to a Sceptic',[1] in the Wentworth Woodhouse MSS.

No. 18, 'Dialogue', on the other hand, contains little specifically characteristic of Edmund's thought or manner, and may perhaps be by William, though some of its satire echoes certain passages in *The Reformer*. Its authorship must, however, remain doubtful.

No. 20, 'Some Political...Observations', undoubtedly contains passages very typical of Edmund's thought and style; for example, ' Of [*sic*] Papist to be a protestant, it is only necessary to throw off something; from Pr[otestant] to become papist something must be assumed'; and indeed the whole of the passage about Protestants and Papists. Or again 'Great Subtelities and Refinements of reasoning are like Spirits drawn from Liquors; which disorder the Brain, and are much less useful than the ordinary Liquors, tho of a grosser Nature'. On the other hand the last two sections of the piece are less typical of Edmund. But on the whole we would attribute it to him.

No. 24, 'Voltaire', may well be by Edmund, though it consists of little more than a few hastily written notes on certain passages in the authors criticised, for the passage 'Does it prove that the tartars...? Does it prove that the Anglo Saxons...? Does the great Empire of Attila prove...?' is certainly typical of what we may term Burke's cumulative rhetoric; while we know from *The Annual Register*, and from his later writings on the French Revolution, that Edmund knew Voltaire's works well. But perhaps William Burke did also. Its authorship must remain doubtful.

Thus from internal evidence it would appear that the authorship of nos. 18 and 24 is doubtful, but that no. 20 is very probably by Edmund, and that nos. 13, 14, 15, 16 and 17 are almost certainly by him.

[1] This manuscript is an account of what Burke replied to a sceptic.

Meanwhile we may note that extracts from the note-book have already been printed on eight occasions: first, by James Prior in his *Memoir of the Life and Character of the Right Hon. Edmund Burke*; second, by the present writer in *The Times* of 12 January 1938, under the title 'New Burke Papers: The "Character of a Good Man"'; third, by the present writer in *The Times Educational Supplement* of 10 December 1938 under the title 'Burke on Education: a "Find"'; fourth, by the late Professor Dixon Wecter of the University of Colorado in an essay entitled 'The Missing Years in Edmund Burke's Biography', in the *Publications of the Modern Language Association* of December 1938; fifth, by the present writer in an article entitled 'Edmund Burke Outside Politics' in *The Dublin Review* of January 1939; sixth, by the late Professor Dixon Wecter in his study *Edmund Burke and his Kinsmen*, published as Vol. 1 of University of Colorado Studies in February 1939; seventh, by Sir Philip Magnus, Bart., in his *Edmund Burke* in 1939; and eighth by Monsieur Paul Baratier of the University of Grenoble in the revue *Études Anglaises* (Didier, Paris) for April 1954 and for January–March 1955.

Prior's quotation consists of 'The Character of — [Mrs Burke]', down to the words 'beautiful of hers', only omitting the last short and rather touching paragraph. The article in *The Times* of 12 January 1938 consists of some parts only of 'The Character of a Good Man', illustrating, as it was thought, Burke's own character. The article in *The Times Educational Supplement* quotes various passages on education from the 'Several Scattered Hints Concerning Philosophy and Learning collected here from my Papers'. The essay of Dixon Wecter, of December 1938, contains a short account of the note-book, and some quotations from the poems as illustrating the early period of Burke's life in London, 'the missing years' in his biography. The article in the *Dublin Review* of January 1939 quotes various passages from the note-book as showing the early development of some of Burke's characteristic habits of thought. Dixon Wecter's *Edmund Burke and his Kinsmen* contains a number of extracts from the note-book 'to illustrate the character of youthful philosophising of the future statesman'— namely the whole of 'The Character of a Fine Gentleman', some more quotations from his poems, an allusion to 'A Letter to Sir James Lowther', an extract from 'Phidippus' (the character of William Burke), and allusions to 'The Way to Preferment', to 'Several Political Scattered Observations', to 'The Character of a Wise Man', and to 'The Character of a Good Man'. Sir Philip Magnus in his biography of Burke quotes, like Prior, 'The Character of — [Mrs Burke]'. Monsieur Baratier gives 'The Character of a Good Man', 'The Character of a Wise Man', and 'Several Scattered Hints concerning Philosophy and Learning'.

Such would seem to be the sum of the quotations so far published from the note-book, the whole of which is here printed for the first time.

Burke wrote a good deal 'outside politics' in addition to what is to be found of that nature in the note-book. His well-known *Vindication of Natural Society* (1756) may be considered as of that character, to the extent that it is an imitation of the literary style of Bolingbroke; he collaborated with William Burke in the *Account of the European Settlements in America* (1757); he achieved considerable fame before he entered politics with his *Enquiry into our Ideas of the Sublime and Beautiful* (1757) upon which he is said to have been working before he left Trinity College, Dublin;[1] he added to this an essay on 'Taste' in the second edition (1759); sometime before 1765 he wrote an unfinished sketch entitled *Hints for an Essay on the Drama*; he also published an *Abridgment of the English History*; and while still in Dublin he had printed a number of

[1] See Samuels, *Early Life, Correspondence and Writings.*

miscellaneous essays in his own weekly periodical *The Reformer* (1747–8);[1] he had published a number of poems, including a translation of Virgil's second *Georgic* in a composite volume entitled *Poems on Several Occasions* (Dublin, 1748);[2] and, later, in *The Annual Register*, the first number of which he produced in 1758, he devoted a considerable portion of each volume to 'Characters', 'Literary and Miscellaneous Essays', 'Poetry', and other non-political subjects.

In comparing some of these with the note-book we find that his twelve pieces from *The Reformer* consist of an Introductory Essay[3] with some verses, and essays on (a) the degenerate state of the theatre; (b) plays; (c) the need for patronage of the arts; (d) coffee-house talk; (e) the state of learning and poetry; (f) the state of Ireland's poor, and 'the luxurious lives of its gentry'; (g) the vulgarity of comic actors; (h) some comedies; (i) religion and morality; (j) the error of making 'spirit' not sense the essence of good writing;[4] and (k) false criticism in general;—and in these essays several subjects, and indeed several phrases bear a close analogy to passages in the note-book.[5]

In *The Annual Register* also there are a number of poems, essays, and 'characters', not necessarily by himself, closely comparable with the contents of the note-book. We have, for instance, in the first number in 1758 (under the heading 'Characters') 'The King of Prussia' by Maupertuis, 'Voltaire, said to have been written by a P—ce',[6] and the characters of Lord

---

[1] Cf. p. 7 above. His contributions to the Lucas controversy we omit, since these were of a political character.

[2] See Samuels, *op. cit.*

[3] 'The Design...', he writes, 'of these Papers is carefully and impartially to examine, not only those Writings which may be produced among ourselves, or imported from abroad, but also our Theatrical Amusements' (Samuels, p. 277).

[4] Cf. 'The Man of Spirit' in this note-book.

[5] E.g. see p. 7 above on no. 14 of the note-book.

[6] Frederick the Great, no doubt.

Somers and others, taken from Swift; and, under the heading of 'Literary and Miscellaneous Essays', 'Essay on Taste' by Montesquieu. In 1759, characters of Clarendon (by Burke himself?), of General Wolfe—'generous almost to profusion' (a very Burke-like phrase)—of Ben Jonson, Mrs Siddons, Edmund Waller, and others; and also a 'Singular Account of a Miser', with which we may compare the 'Letter to Sir James Lowther, a very Notorious Miser' in the note-book;[1] and, under the heading of Miscellaneous Essays, 'The Advantages of Ancestry Demonstrated' (again a very Burke-like subject), 'On Biography' (from *The Idler*), and 'An Essay on Monosyllables'. In 1760, under the heading 'Miscellaneous Essays', we find, in an essay entitled 'Various Thoughts on Various Subjects', several phrases reminiscent of the note-book, such as, for instance, 'Learning, like Money, is not an end but a means...' (p. 206),[2] and 'He that lives in a college, after his mind is sufficiently stocked with learning, is like a man, who having built and rigged and victualled a ship, should lock her up in a dry dock' (*ibid.*),[3] and 'refined and elegant sensibility is a shorter way to rectitude than reason' (*ibid.*).[4] In 1761, moreover, we find the 'Character of a good sort of woman' from *The Idler*, and also a 'Character of a mighty good kind of man', which is also interesting, since it was almost certainly written by William Burke; for it contains the phrase 'I remember at Westminster, *a mighty good kind of boy*, though he was generally hated by his school'; and we know that William Burke was himself educated at Westminster. Here, then, apparently is William Burke collaborating with Edmund in *The Annual Register*, just as he collaborated with him in the note-book.

[1] See below, no. 9, p. 49.
[2] Cf. below, no. 19, p. 82. 'To study only for its own sake is a fruitless labour' and *passim*.
[3] Cf. *ibid*.          [4] Cf. p. 8, no. 17 above.

Indeed one could continue almost indefinitely to draw analogies between the note-book and *The Annual Register*. But the point need not be laboured. Suffice it to say that both show the extent of Burke's interest in matters outside politics.

Another sphere in which Burke's wide literary, scientific, moral and religious interests were exhibited—though not in writing but in speaking—was, of course, that of the College Historical Society at Trinity College, Dublin, of which a full account is given in Samuel's book; and here we find the members, and among them prominently Burke himself, debating, or writing on, a great variety of themes, as well as declaiming famous passages of poetry and of oratory.

The following, for example, are some of the subjects upon which Burke debated: on the Genoese; on the recent conduct of the Dutch; on the recent conduct of the English; on 'the advantages England would receive by the Prince of Orange being made Stadtholder'; on 'whether Philosophy be of use to poetry'; on 'a bill to tax absentee landlords'; on 'ye figure of the Eclyptick'; on piracy in printing; on the expulsion of Coriolanus; on 'the law that makes sheep stealing death'; on 'whether the Turkish law that forbids wine, be just'; and we find Burke speaking, in the character of General Huske, on 'engaging the rebels at Falkirk', in the character of Brutus the first, on the death of Lucretia; in the character of a Roman senator, against Caesar setting out for Gaul; in the character of Ulysses, on 'the embassy of Ulysses and Menelaus to receive Helen'; in the character of a Roman senator, against the return of Regulus to Carthage;—and also declaiming such pieces as Moloch's speech from *Paradise Lost* (Book II, ll. 50 *et seq.*) and Othello's speech to the senate;—'lecturing' on oratory;—and writing essays on such subjects as 'Society',[1] 'Malice', 'the earthquake at Lima', 'Discretion', etc.: while papers read by other members of the Society include such subjects as

[1] Cf. his later 'Vindication of Natural Society'.

'Poverty', 'Love', 'Drunkenness', 'Luxury', 'Pride', 'austere and chearful [sic] religion', 'Charity', and 'Satire'—subjects which bear a close relationship to those later treated by Burke in the London note-book.

Meanwhile we may consider what preparation for literary work Burke had made during his student days at Trinity College, Dublin, which he entered in April 1744 at the age of fifteen, and which he left, in order to proceed to the Middle Temple, early in 1750. What had been his education during this period, whether supplied by his teachers or by his own private reading?

The outline of the degree course for a student at Trinity, in his time, was officially as follows. In the first year he was to study rhetoric and logic; in the second controversial logic; in the third natural science; and in the fourth psychology and ethics. The set books in the first two years included Virgil, Horace, Juvenal, Tacitus, Suetonius, Homer, Sophocles, Demosthenes, Xenophon (the *Cyropedia* only), and Longinus, for rhetoric; and the *Institutiones Logicae* of Burgersdicius (first published in 1626), the *Logica, sive Ars ratiocinandi* of Le Clerc (a French Protestant theologian, editions of whose work were published in English in 1692 and in 1702), and parts of the *Logica of Smiglecius* (first published in 1618), for Logic;—though in the works both of Burgersdicius (a Dutch professor of Leyden) and of Smiglecius (a Polish Jesuit) were contained 'a good deal of grammar and metaphysics' [1] in addition to purely formal logic.

For the third year the books set were Wells' *Astronomy*, the *Universal Geography* of Varenius, and part of the *Physica* of Le Clerc—the last covering astronomy, geology, geography, meteorology, biology and mechanics, as well as what we under-

---

[1] See the article by R. B. McDowell and D. A. Webb on 'Courses and Teaching in Trinity College, Dublin, during the first 200 years' in *Hermathena*, no. LXIX (Dublin, 1947), to which we owe most of our information on the subject of the Dublin degree course.

stand by physics today; though the student's attention was probably chiefly directed to the mechanics and physics.[1]

For the fourth—and final—year the books set were the *Ethics* of Eustachius (a French Cistercian who died in 1613), the *Metaphysics* of Baronius (a professor of Divinity of Aberdeen who died in 1639), the *Prelections* of Sanderson (Regius Professor of Divinity at Oxford, 1646–7, and later Bishop of Lincoln), and '*the small Pufendorf*' of the German scholar and historian of that name (born 1632, died 1694).

Such was the normal course of reading at Trinity College at this time. But we know that Burke was also acquainted with the *Enchiridion* of Epictetus, with the *Tabula* of Cebes, with Terence and Plautus, and with some Aristotle; and that he was 'examined for two days in all the Roman and Greek authors of note',[2] and more particularly in Sallust, when competing for the scholarship which he secured in May 1746.

In his first year, also, he is found attending a course of lectures by one John Booth in Natural Science, and pursuing many other intellectual interests outside the college curriculum —particularly in the last two years of his residence; for during this period we find that he mentions a number of books and authors not included in his official studies, for example, Shakespeare, Beaumont and Fletcher, Voiture, Waller, Cowley, Otway, Addison, Pope, Hammond, and the old romances *Don Bellianis of Greece* and *Palmerin of England*; and that he spends almost three hours every day in the public library—at one time 'far gone in the poetical madness', next 'turning back to logic and 'metaphysics', and then given up to 'the *furor historicus*'—'endeavouring to get a little into the accounts of this our own poor country', or immersed in the history of France and of Naples; and at one time attending a course on optics;

---

[1] McDowell and Webb, *loc. cit.*

[2] Burke had won 'the thanks of ye House' for 'diligence at Greek Lecture' in 1744, and also obtained a prize for Greek in 1745 (Samuels, p. 55).

and at another obtaining 'a ticket to attend Dr Bailie's lectures on the Civil Law'.

Moreover, it is particularly significant, in relation to the note-book, to observe how deeply interested he is in 'characters', writing, for instance, in 1746, 'I have, I know not how, got into the trade of character drawing'; and in another place, observing, in praising Sallust, 'Neither should I pass by his beautiful painting of characters.'[1]

But we have already pointed out how prominently 'characters' figure later in *The Annual Register*, and we shall here only add that E. J. Payne in the Introduction to his edition of Burke's *Select Works* observes that 'Burke employed with great effect the device...of diversifying his writings by the introduction of what are called "characters". The characters of Grenville, Charles Townshend, of the Chatham Ministry, and of the American Colonists, are specimens, so also Walpole, Montesquieu, Fox, Saville, Howard, and others.'[2] He might have added also that of Admiral Keppel.[3]

Evidently, then, Burke was deeply influenced by the long tradition of character drawing in English literature, from Joseph Hall's *Characters of Vertues and Vices* (1608), through Samuel Butler, Stephens, Fuller, Overbury, Lupton—with his *London and the Countrey Carbonadoed and Quartered into severall Characters*—Clarendon, Halifax and the translators of Theophrastus and of La Bruyère, down to Chesterfield and others in his own time;[4] and the characters in the note-book, we venture to think, are not unworthy of that tradition.

[1] Samuels, p. 129.
[2] Quoted by Samuels, p. 105; cf. also Wecter in *P.M.L.A.* (1939) on 'Characters of the Fine Gentleman in English Writings'.
[3] Cf. also Fanny Burney's glowing account of Burke expanding in conversation on the character of Cardinal Ximenes (Madame d'Arblay, *Memoirs of Dr Burney*, 1832).
[4] See C. N. Greenough, *A Bibliography of the Theophrastan Character* (Harvard University Press, 1947).

Burke, then, was well prepared, both by his course of studies at Trinity and by his own independent self-education[1] to become an author in 1750, the date of the first of the pieces printed here. Indeed he himself later avowed that his mind was at the height of its power to discuss abstract questions during his residence at Trinity; and, as we have already noted, it was almost certainly at this time that he composed most—or all— of his *Enquiry into our Ideas of the Sublime and Beautiful,* a work which, as Lord Morley has pointed out,[2] was of considerable importance in the history of aesthetics, and largely influenced Lessing in his *Laocoon.* How different, too, was the intense course of study imposed upon Burke and his contemporaries at Dublin from the lax and careless character of the education—if such indeed it can be called—provided at Oxford at this time, and castigated by Gibbon in a famous passage of his *Autobiography.* No wonder that Johnson later said of Burke that 'his stream of mind was perpetual'; for even by the time he came to London he had already drunk deep of the Pierian spring.

Thus it is not surprising that, if some portions of the notebook are little more than studies and exercises in logic, natural science, satire and apologetics, yet in a number of other passages can already be recognised many of the essential characteristics of the future statesman and greatest of British political philosophers.

[1] Cf. Burke in 1780 in his speech on declining the poll at Bristol. 'I have read the book of life for a long time, and I have read other books a little' (Almon, *Anecdotes,* vol. III, App. p. 407).

[2] Quoted by Samuels, p. 137.

# A NOTE-BOOK OF
# EDMUND BURKE

## NOTE

In this edition of Burke's note-book we have retained his original use of capital letters, but, in the interest of clarity, have revised the punctuation. As an example of our method we may note that in no. 18 the original contains the following passage in the following form:

'You ought to do as I did, not with a serious face but as in drollery it is like a mountebank, and his merry Andrew one acts sillily in a grave way and the other in a brisk now they are both blockheads....'

which we have rendered:

'You ought to do as I did, not with a serious face, but as in drollery. It is like a mountebank and his Merry Andrew. One acts sillily in a grave way, and the other in a brisk. Now they are both blockheads....'

## 1

This piece shows Burke divided between his love of literature and his need to concentrate on his legal studies; and thus throws some light on what the late Professor Dixon Wecter termed 'the missing years in Edmund Burke's biography'.

∾

## THE MUSE DIVORCED

An Epistle from Mr E. Burke to his friend
Mr W. Burke

CROYDON                                    NOVEMBER 1750

His Life who changes has a Deal to do
To break old habits, and establish new;
His nature rises for the good old cause,
His little Kingdom will assert its Laws;
Custom opposes; pride itself is strong;
We own, by Changing, that we once were wrong.
Our Interest sometimes we're induced to part;
Our Vanity grows nearer to the Heart.
This felt a grave Divine as well as we,
Who, not to Damn his Book, renounc'd his see.
Full half his Laurels Richlieu would resign,
O Envied Corneille, for one Branch of thine.
Whoe'er has faults, and chuses not to mend,
By great examples may his faults defend.
But I whose Ardor thinking daily cools,
And time has taught,—for time e'en teaches fools,—
Galled with the straitness of the Marriage Noose,
Tho' late, did thus repudiate my Muse:
'Hence from my Doors! begone! I set thee free!
Take all the portion I receiv'd with thee!

All the vain hopes of Profit and of praise;
The blasted Ivy and the Hungry Bays;
The time ill spent or lost (the Dreamer's lot)
The Idle Learning, which I wish forgot,—
The high romantick flights, the mad Designs,
Th'unnumbered number of neglect^d Lines,
The Itch, that first to scribbling turn'd my Quill,
The fatal Itch, that makes me scribble still.
Take these, and all the relicts of thy store;—
The rich in that, are poorest of the Poor.
Go! and may better fate thy steps attend!
Go! and learn better how to chuse a friend—
Some Fop whose pride and vast Estate admit,
The Weighty charge of Idleness and Wit.'
Thus whilst I spoke, my better Genius led;
And yet anon I wish'd it all unsaid.
The poet's ail no Remedies can ease,
Because we cherish still our own disease;
What e'er the Turn of mind stills ^1 verse presents;
Here all the Passions have their Proper vents.
Are we Enraged? revenge presents us soon
The murdering Dagger of a keen Lampoon:
If proud—in Lofty Odes we tread the Sky,
Swell in Heroics, strut in Tragedy—:
If the soft impulse of Desire we prove,
What so ally'd as Poetry and Love?
If, wiser grown, we would redeem our time,
'Tis but good manners to take leave in Rhime.
If we succeed, success gives cause t' indite;
If we should fail, Despair provokes to write.
The strong and weak consume in the same fire,
The force unequal, equal the Desire.
What Whips! What Stings! what furies drive us on?

^1 Meaning 'distils'.

22

Why all this Mighty rage to be undone?
Why still persist when ruin and Disgrace,
When want and Shame present their hideous face?
When scornful Silence loudly cries, Abstain,
Our friends advise, our parents preach in vain.
Well, sage Astrologers, I yield at Last;
I own the folly of my Wisdom past.
Your Convert grown, with Rev'rence I reflect
On time, and Quartile,[1] and Malign Aspect.
What e'er the stars determine at our Birth,
Whether to conquer, or to Plough the Earth;
Whether to wear the Ribband or the Rope;
Whether to be, or whether burn, a Pope;
Whether in gouty Pride on down to loll,
Or Range with Midnight whores the cold patrol;
This Rules our Days; in vain the Wretch would fly:—
His Stars o'erlook him with a conscious Eye;
Drag back the Rebel to his destined State,
The Chain refusing, strugling with his fate.
E'en I, while arming for the wordy War,
Neglect the spoils and trophies of the Bar,
Drawn by th'attraction of my natal Ray;—
Against my Reason often Quit my way.
Yet preach to others in the same distress;
Dissuade with Words, and then dissuade no less
By sad Example of my own success.
Oh, what a Shameful Fate does he endure
Who sees his fault, and seeing cannot cure!
When scenes like these afflict the tortured Soul,
Say, is the Lynx more happy than the mole?
Yet sure he happy is—or happy none—

[1] 'The aspect of two heavenly bodies which are 90° distant from each other'
*O.E.D.* 'The Heavens threaten us with their...oppositions, quartiles, and such unfriendly aspects' (Burton, *Anatomy of Melancholy*).

Whose choice and Interest in one Channel run.
His greatest toils his greatest pleasures prove:—
For how can Labour weary which we love?
On all he Acts propitious Venus smiles;
And Graces weave their Dance among his toils.

He's happy too, who lets no care Destroy
The Prosp'rous moment of the present Joy.
The hopeful parson new arriv'd in town,
Who just has got a wife, and just a Gown,
Tho' young yet rev'rend, warm yet Nice in Love,
Enjoys chaste raptures with his Turtle Dove.
What pretty Chat! What soft endearing Arts!
What blending souls! What Sympathy of Hearts!
Mindless, the while, of Duns' impatient calls,
The Grocer's hooks, the Victler's fouler scrawls,
And Chandler's endless Scores that Whiten all the Walls.
*This swain, if Nature to the Test we bring,
Tastes more true joy, and nearer to the spring,
Than we who, vainly wise, consume our years
Ills to prevent, that only mock our Cares;
Or tho' our fortunes our desires should Shape,
Gain all we wish, and all we fear escape.
In this alone, my friend, true Quiet lies,
Wholly to be a fool, or wholly wise.
The space betwixt is but a mangled Scene;
Here the Extreams are Golden, not the mean.
Those hapless Lands that warring Realms divide,
By turns are wasted by the conquering side.
A like or worse Distraction we shall find
In minds so mixed, in Contraries so join'd;—

* These Lines allude to Mr C., a very honest Young Divine very much in
Love and more in Debt. Very Orthodox and very Poor. [Perhaps referring
to Churchill?]

While folly's dreams are still by Wisdom cross'd,
And wisdom's Schemes by Headstrong folly Lost.
With great Designs a fickle mind ill suits;
An equal Sky must ripen generous fruits.
Under whatever Standard we Inlist,
T'were better ne'er begin, than not persist.

Rous'd with these thoughts I lash my Lazy side,
And all my strength collect and all my Pride;
All boyish dreams for ever disavow;
Then dream, and Triffle, play, and rhime as now.
This of myself I know, and more amiss;
But should Will Burke presume to tell me this,—
The Fool! the Coxcomb, the ill mannered Elf!
Who dares to think me—What I think myself.
Can we, my friend, with any Conscience bear,
To show our minds sheer naked as they are,
Remove each veil of Custom, pride or Art,
Nor stretch a hand to hide one Shameful part?—
An equal Share of Scorn and Danger find
A Naked body, and an open mind.
Both sights unusual; sights which never fail
To make the Witty laugh, and pious Rail.
The Children fly for fear; the women scream;
And Sages cry the World has Lost its Shame.

And ev'n some friends—that sacred Name—we have,
Whom so to keep, 'tis proper to deceive;
Who Lofty Notions build on Plato's plan,
And grow quite angry when they find you *man*.
Who can be friends, and yet be Judges too?
Few can be such. Then Let me keep those few.

## 2

William Burke here replies to the foregoing by bidding Edmund not
to desert his Muse altogether, but to cultivate her for the benefit of
himself and his friends—

    'Thy Muse's Voice shall Gladden every Guest,
    Your heart be hers, in her be all your joy;
    But Let the law your Graver thoughts employ....
    Preserve your Pen for good, but private Ends;
    T'amuse yourself, Instruct and Charm your friends.'

~·

## THE ANSWER TO IT

An Epistle to Mr E. Burke from Mr W. Burke in
answer to the foregoing

LONDON                             NOVEMBER 1750

A Scripture Curse on him denounced we find
Who separates those that Heaven's Decree hath join'd,
With ties as close, with Bonds no less divine,
Poet and muse in Mystick Concert join;
What fearless Wretch so daring, then, to break
That sacred League which Heav'n alone can make?
Such bonds you surely cannot wish to loose!
I ne'er advis'd, nor must you part your Muse;
When fearfull Cully, makes his Punk a Wife,[1]
Or Grave-like Matron takes a Rake for Life,
Where no Consent appears, no Mark of Love,
Can we suppose such Leagues are made above?
So I, and hundreds more in Rhymes may end
Our Lines, and vainly call each Muse our Friend.
Fearless may all between such Couples go,

  [1] Alluding to some marriages that then were much talked of.

26

For surely Heaven had nothing there to do.
But when the Poet's Tragic fire shall raise
Alternate Terror, Pity and Amaze,
And shews us falling in his Country's Cause
An Hero fearless of a Tyrant's Laws,
Who envy'd thus, resignes his patriot Breath
And makes us wish his virtues, to deserve his Death,
Or when strong Satire,[1] rough indeed but true,
Our hateful Self lays open to our View;
Where th'hand Divine is markt with such a force,
T'were Sacriledge to mention a Divorce.
Tho' Claret flow not at thine humble feast,
Thy Muse's Voice shall Gladden every Guest;
Your heart be hers, in her be all your joy;
But Let the law your Graver thoughts employ;
That you for Life may still her fav'rite prove;
For if you'r poor you'll surely lose her Love.
Your word, Dear friend, has been my guiding Line,
Your Conduct was, and is the Rule of mine;
And this is all my boast, I now advise,[2]
But not through Vanity of seeming Wise.
Preserve your Pen for good, but private Ends;
T'amuse yourself, Instruct and Charm your friends.

[1] Alluding to a satire of Mr E.B.'s to whom the Epistle is addressed.
[2] [ = My only boast is that I am your adviser?]

## 3

This piece is surely not good enough to justify Walpole's and Almon's tributes to William Burke's powers (see Introduction, p. 3).

⌁

## THE PILLOW. BY W.B.

An Epistle to Doctor Nugent who never used a Pillow

OXFORD                                                                    JUNE 1753

Thou! sweetest Comfort of a *Dunsick mind
Thou! soft and easy Pillow, still art kind.
Since when I left the friends that love me best,
In thee and thee alone I've found true rest.
Cease Lovers cease, your Phillis now give o'er,
Your flames, your Darts, your Raptures, vaunt no more.
For who is She, so soft, so neat, so fair,
As you, my gently yielding Pillow, are?
Let Learning Lift its Vot'ries to the Skies,
And Wisdom teach above the World to rise;
Yet come a frost, will wisdom keep them warm?
Received by thee what Frost can do me harm?
Let friends to Wealth point out the Anxious road,
You ease my Mind of Recollection's load,
While on your Bosom I enraptured lie,
And Care, and Pain, and Poverty Defy.
But lives there one who dares thy Power disown,
And Slights the Charms of thy Lethean Down?
Were there indeed a man whose youthfull Day

---

* Mr W.B. the Author was then not a little pestered by a [numerous] band of Creditors, who were very little satisfyed with good words, and Mr B. had no money for them and used to retire to his pillow when they wearied him out.

Was journey'd out, through Learning's various way,
In Wisdom's search; whose Age, not Idle grown,
Now reaps the fruit, his Carefull Youth had sown,
And yet whose Learning is his meanest Part,
Whose greatest Good, whose chiefest Virtue is his Heart;—
His worth he cannot in himself confine,
It spreads with goodly Wing through all his Line;—
A Sister who with manly force sustains
A loaded life of sorrows, Cares and Pains,—
Whate'er her lot, she ne'er repines at fate,
She never weeps but when a friend's unfortunate—
A Daughter[1] form'd each Ill of Life t'assuage,
And sooth with lenient hands the Cares of Age,
Whose Love and Duty join their friendly hands;—
She ne'er obeys, because he ne'er commands.
I grant if such a man you ever see,
He may without a Pillow happy be.

[ 4 ]

A rather strained piece of humorous verse. We have not been able
to discover the meaning of 'Hessing' in the fifth line from the end.

❧

## AN ANSWER TO THE PILLOW.
### BY E.B.

BATH                                              JULY 1753

      Let no more of Bays be said;
      Let a Pillow bind my Head.
      For 'tis now by merit grown
      Much more splendid than a Crown.

[1] Jane Nugent, the future Mrs Edmund Burke. Cf. nos. 10 and 11.

Oh could I, by magic skill,
Turn each feather to a quill!
Then in lofty verse I'd tell
That your Pillow does excell
All the streams of Pindus' well;
That all those who write for fame
Should upon your Pillow dream,
Not on Parnass' forked head;
Maugre what Old Bards have said.
Fired with true poetick rapture
I soar into an Higher Chapter;
And Lo! I see your Pillow rise,
Wafted to the admiring Skies;
Set a star[1] within the sphere
Close by Bernice's hair;
Or within the Zodiac Snug,
For th'old Virgin there to hug;
Or near Cuckold Capricorn's,
To repose his aking horns.
Long it shall propitious show
To poor Dunsick Minds below;
Or to Debtors give Delight,
Showing thro' Ludgate Bars its Light;
Or direct the odorous Feet
Of Quinbus Flestrin[2] in the fleet.
To Creditors it shall portend
Statutes of Bankcruptcies in the end;

[1] I.e. set as a star.

[2] See *Gulliver's Travels*, I, ch. 2, where Quinbus Flestrin is stated to be the Lilliputian for 'Great Man-Mountain': but see below, p. 40.

See also Pope and Swift, *Miscellanies* (1727), III, pp. 274–5, where there is a short poem 'To Quinbus Flestrin the Man-Mountain, a Lilliputian Ode'. Cf. also Christopher Smart's poem *The Hilliad* (1753), a satire on Dr John Hill, 'the Inspector' (see no. 7 below, p. 40), to which notes are contributed by Quinbus Flestrin. It is not clear to whom the name refers in these literary pieces.

To Constables and such Damned fellows,
Carrion and Newgate and the Gallows;
To poor Nymphs shall point the route,
When fallacious Lamps are out;
While wits and Lawyers safe shall trample
Without the Purlieus of the Temple.
In short shall be the star of Blessing
To Debt and Poetry and Hessing.
Long may it rain its influence
O'er us who feel the want of Pence,
While Rich Rogues shall waste their Days
Without Pillow, without Praise.

[ 5 ]

This piece would seem to have something of the 'ingenuity and sharpness' which Horace Walpole noted in William Burke's writings (see Introduction, p. 3).

∾

## AN EPISTOLARY ESSAY ON THE NATURAL HISTORY OF A BUCK

TURLAINE                                    SEP[TEMBER] 1754

[By William Burke]

Dear Sir,

When last I had the pleasure of being in your Company, and I declare I cannot have a greater, among other Philosophical Inquirys *The Buck*, a Creature the Antients knew as little of as of Lamas, and Tacunas, became the Subject of our conversation.

I believe Newton and Des Cartes differed not more widely about Light and Colours than a friend of ours and I did in our opinions of this Creature called *Buck—Sed ne te morer audi*

31

*quo rem Deducam* [1]—without particularly answering the objections of others, I will give you my own Opinion, which, if it is not a Philosophical Way, is at least the way of many Philosophers.

We find it written,—I need not, sir, to you quote Page and Vol.—that in early times the country Gentleman, that is the man who had a good Estate in the Country, seldom or never saw the Town; But spending his money among his Tenants, in the Country he there lived and there he died.

If we wanted any stronger proof of this, we need but recollect what Tradition assures us of, that the distant roads from London were almost impassable; so that few dared venture them. And sure 'Illi Robur et aes triplex circa pectus erat'— who first dared these Wiltshire Hills e'er Turnpikes had pav'd the way. Before that time the freeholder, withheld by Bad Roads as by *Oceano dissociabili* from Town, was happy and content in what he found on his own Land. He looked no farther; but joyfully followed his Hounds and tilled his Acres. And thus our forefathers dwelled in peace. Their braver Sons, not content with common sport, increas'd the Game; and with equal Might and Honour run down Hares, Foxes, and Milkmaids. And this Creature was known by the name of Foxhunter.

I have no sooner brought you acquainted with this Creature, than I must desire you to leave him awhile in the Woods and take a view of what was doing in Town.

Montesquieu is of opinion that the Climate affects, or rather causes the Dispositions, of the mind.—Torrid and frigid are not more opposite and Different than were then Country and Town. No wonder, then, if this Latter produced a Creature quite unlike the other. Both indeed pursued their pleasures, but their pleasures were as unlike as themselves. The first was

[1] The MS. is here clearly corrupt: it should probably read 'Sed ne temere aliquam rem deducam'.

always in Action. To pursue his pleasure he was every Morning before the sun. The other suffered the sun to run half its Course before he appeared. But was he found in bed at noon? He made ample amends for not rising early by not going to bed till very Late. Women and wine engrossed his time and thoughts. Yet then—but let me stop from drawing this Character, as it does not Directly tend to my Point; and as Mr Steel has already wrote his Apology, imagine not, Sir, that I think he wants excuse, when I say we have his apology; For remember, we have Socrates Apology as well as the *Rakes*;—for so was this Creature called.

The Foxhunter and Rake for a long time remained separated;—The Rake from the fox hunter, and the fox hunter from the Rake; and each produced their Like. The time and means that brought them together are somewhat Difficult to ascertain. But in all Philosophical enquirys Conjecture must be allowed sometimes. Politicks, that so often divides, was what, I conjecture, first reconciled these different Natures. What inclines me to think so is, that I do not find either Rake or foxhunter among the round heads; so that it is Likely they were both in loyal Banishment with the King, and after the Restoration both perhaps met at Court; each looking for the rewards of their services. The king's peculiar turn, who was fond of a variety of Characters, and who, as he indulged himself in all the Court pleasure, was also fond of Hunting and Races, might have encouraged this Union. In short,—how it happened let wiser Naturelists account but—certainly they came together, joined, and Produced a new species, known in our Days by the name of a Buck; and neither Rake or Foxhunter are more heard of among us.

The Buck, then, is an Amphibeous creature; in utrumque paratus—to break Lamps in Covent Garden or his own neck over a five Barr'd Gate in the Country.

A Buck must have a good Deal of money, ought to have a

strong Constitution, and must think a little;—just enough to make him repent heartily of all he does; and yet must have such an easiness of Temper as to be persuaded to do the same things over and over again. A Buck need not be very Learned, But must not be an Ignorant. Whatever he does that is outree[1] must be owing to that Easiness of Temper that I mentioned before. Whether this easiness of Temper deserves the name of good Nature or not, I won't say; and yet it must make him assist his Companion and always ready to relieve the Distressed. A proneness to expense, a total disregard of money, are inseparable incidents in his Character. In short, it may be a Paradox, Yet an easiness of Temper, and strong passions are the Characteristick of a Buck. The first will make him acceptable everywhere; and that he may be so, is one Reason why he must not be an Ignorant; the other—his strong passions—will assist the Persuasions of those whose Company he, in his Interval[s] of thought, so often repented. But 'tis the very Essence of a Buck that those Intervals should be very Short; they must indeed be over as soon as his Breakfast.

I promised in the beginning to give you my own Opinion; and so I intended. But my Opinion is just changed; and I fear I must own the Life of a Buck is a Life of folly and Repentance, Repentance and folly. And in return you'll, I believe, agree that these Follys may be forgiven if they are given over before 'tis too late for our friends to say—'he is young'. Well, my dear friend, I have wearied you—deny it not; for I own I am very Sleepy. So I'll go to Bed. And the last wish I make, unless the Devil puts some wicked thought across me, shall be for your Health and Happiness; which I shall always wish while I have a grain of Sense or Honesty. And when I have not, you'll be weak enough to Pity me.

W. D.

[1] *outré.*

This is another contribution to our knowledge of 'the missing years' and of Burke's character as a young man.

∾

## AN EPISTLE TO DOCTOR NUGENT.
### BY E.B.

TURLAINE[1]                                            SEPR. 1751

A grave Philosopher, whom Fate had thrown
'Midst all the Busy Bustle of the Town,
Could never Compass his exalted Views,
While this of stocks enquires, and that of News.
His thoughts are broken with discordant Sounds;
An Almanacks Cry, an Epocha confounds.[2]
Just as he finds what Long his Labours crosst,
An Idle friend pops in, and all is Lost.
To Courts and Alleys then in vain he flies;
For Courts and Alleys have their louder Cries.
Such were his days, but were his nights secure?
The barbarous watchman thunders at the Door.
Tormented thus, he pants for rural Shades;
The thoughtful Coverts, and the silent glades;
To draw from rivulets that murmur there,
From ancients Books, calm Sleep, and frugal fare,
The sweet oblivion of a Life of Care.
Suppose him now in a sequestered Grot;
Deep, very Deep, into the Country Got;

[1] Evidently the modern Turleigh in Wiltshire; it is found spelt Turlyn in 1748. *Vide* the English Place-Name Society's volume for Wiltshire.
[2] The cry of a seller of almanacks confounds.

For none can think, 'tis by the Learn'd confess'd,
Unless from Town full fifty Leagues at Least.
First, then, Rome's Centinels proclaim the Day;
An hundred Cocks salute the Morning Gray;
The Rooks a Clamorous Council hold on high,
The oxen low, the fiery Coursers neigh;
A thousand throats awake ten thousand more;
Till Hills, and woods and Vales are all aroar.
What shall our Student do? Why, Shift the Scene,
Pack up his Books and turn to Town again.

This Tale, dear friend, in his own striking way
(murdered by me) you'll meet in Rabelais.
Some end it serves, if it can mirth produce;
It serves a better if it turns to use.
For Solitude is neither here nor there;
Turley's[1] no more retired than Westminster.
In vain we fly from place to place to find
What not in place consists, but in the mind.
If I am fearfull, insolent, or proud,
Or torn with Passions that distract the Croud,
If these I carry to my Country Seat,
Am I in solitude and in Retreat?
But if I feel my soul confirmed and free,
What is the Town, and what the Croud, to me?

As men in pain no posture can abide,
But shift, in hope of Ease, from side to side,
Thus Kings, of Empire sick, of all admired,
From thrones of Care to Convents have retired;
Sick of the Convent too, too late have known
The fault was in themselves and not the Throne.
In vain we strip the Purple from the Skin
If Deeper purple still remains within.

[1] *Vide* p. 35, n. 1.

Perhaps I drive too fast in this Career
And you, good Sir, may whisper in my Ear,
That those who willingly run down a Hill,
Are forced to run yet more against their Will,
So men oft hearted with Conceits they Love,
Prove more, by half, than does them good to prove.

I love retreat, I own; no mortal more.
Shall I applaud my Virtue on that Score?
When, were my Soul laid open to your View,
'Tis more to Indolence than Virtue due.

Heav'n bless those folks, who, seeming to be wise,
With specious names their faults would canonise,
Yet under Planets so perverse are born,
They wish to be the very things they scorn.
That Sage who calls a fop mankind's disgrace
Envies that fop his figure and his face;
That Dame who rails at whores from morn till Night,
Repines that infamy can buy Delight.
And I, who think it is the time's reproach
To see a Scoundrel Gamester in his Coach,
Think modestly t'would have a better Air
To see my humble self exalted there.
Self Love its End pursues by various ways;
We censure others but ourselves to praise.
Why should I list on the severer side?
Will my Own Conduct such a Test abide?
Great Faults we ought in Charity to spare;
And if they're small, they are not worth our Care;
Since from the same contracted notions move
Th'excessive hate of Triffles, and the Love.
I know a man who to th'extreme had brought
The strictest Virtue and the deepest thought;

Who science lov'd, and yet had only trod
The Path of Science as a road to God.
The Arts and Virtues join'd his soul possess'd;
And Taste diffused a Sunshine o'er the rest.
But Art and Taste and Learning only stood
To fill the time he breath'd from doing good.
This man, so grac'd, so little was allied
Or to the Courtly or pedantick pride,
His temper cheerfull, innocent, and free,
Could stoop to all things;—he could stoop to me.
His easy virtue never wore a frown;
He mentioned other's faults as they their own.
Nor even ingenuous follies did he hate;
But left the Proud t'enjoy their sullen State.

*'Tis now two Autumns since he chanc'd to find
A youth of Body broke, infirm of mind.
He gave him all that man can ask or give;
Restor'd his Life, and taught him how to Live.
But what, and when, and How this Youth shall pay,
Must be discuss'd upon a Longer day.
Meantime ten thousand cares distract my Life,
And keep me always with myself at Strife;
Too indolent on flying Wealth to seize;
Of wealth too covetous to be at ease.
I look at Wisdom, wonder, and Adore;
I look, I wonder, but I do no more.
Timrous the Heights of everything I fear;
Perhaps even Wisdom may be bought too Dear.
The Tortoise, snatch'd aloft to highest Air,
Was high, 'tis true, but was not happy there.
Shall I then vapour in a stoic strain,

* Then nineteen his studies had nearly destroyed him. [Note in pencil on the MS.]

38

Who, while I boast, must writhe myself for Pain;
Shall I who grope my way with pur-blind Eyes,—
Shall such as I, pretend to dogmatise?
Better in one low path secure to crawl;
To Doubt of all things, and to Learn from all.

Why should I grieve? In quiet here I dwell—
Our Irish Kings were never lodged so well—
Blest with a friend, with indolence, and peace—
Oh! would kind Heav'n a fortune add to these!
The hopefull end of all my reas'ning see!
Thus have I been and thus shall alway be.
What now I have, I wish'd a year ago;
I have my Wish, and am I happy? No!—
Had I this fortune that I now require,
Is there in Nature nothing to desire?
But providence has more than made amends,
And giv'n what fortune cannot give us—friends.
This pleasing thought yet further to pursue
I want the aid of such a friend as you,
And Hers no less, in whom just Heav'n has joined
The weakest body with the firmest mind.[1]
We'll give you such good Humour as we have;
Nay, I will laugh, William shall be grave.
Our fair and Absent friend we'll toast the while—
(I will not wrong her in this creeping stile).
What would you more? The Skies, the roads are fine;
The sun preparing for the Vernal sign.
Stay if you dare; remember that in Spring
An Angry Poet is a dangerous thing.

[1] Dr Nugent's daughter Jane, the future Mrs Edmund Burke.

[ 7 ]

'The Inspector' was the pseudonym taken by Dr John Hill, M.D.
(Knight of the Swedish Order of Vasa) as author of a series of letters
which he contributed daily for over two years, from March 1751, to
the *London Advertiser and Literary Gazette*. These letters were of a
scurrilous and scandalous character. But Hill went still further in
scurrility in another ephemeral publication entitled *The Impertinent*
in which he maligned several persons, including the poet Christopher Smart, whom he had already praised in *The Inspector*, while he
even developed his double game so far as to make *The Inspector* defend the same persons whom he had already attacked in *The Impertinent*, thus *The Gentleman's Magazine* for August 1751 tells us
that 'The man who thus resents the cruel treatment of Mr Smart in
the Inspector, and he who thus cruelly treated him in the Impertinent is known to be the same'.[1]

The *Hilliad*, 'an Epic Poem by C. Smart A.M....to which are
prefixed Copious Prolegomena and notes variorum, particularly those
of Quinbus Flestrin[2] Esq. and Martinus Macalarius, M.D...',
appeared in 1753. Hill is here hailed as
        'Pimp! Poet! Puffer! Pothecary! Play'r!';
and in fact he was at different times an apothecary, an actor, a play-
wright and a gossip-writer; though his chief work was in the field
of botany and the study of herbs. His most important publications
—and he was author of seventy-six acknowledged works, while
eight more have been attributed to him[3]—was *The Vegetable
System* in twenty-six volumes in folio with 1600 copper-plate en-
gravings representing 26,000 different plants (completed in 1775),
for which he received the Order of Vasa from the King of Sweden.
In this field he did useful work. He also did practical work in
botany, being employed by the Duke of Richmond and by Lord
Petre in arranging their gardens. But in other spheres, though some

[1] Quoted in the prolegomena to Smart's poem *The Hilliad* (1753).
[2] This name occurs in Burke's poem *An Answer to the Pillow*; see above,
p. 30.
[3] See *D.N.B.* under John Hill.

of his plays seem to have had a certain success, he appears chiefly in the guise of a stormy petrel, and centre of scandal and contention. He had violent quarrels with the 'Royal Society', with Fielding, with Smart (as we have seen), and with Garrick; and was 'publicly thrashed at Ranelagh by an Irishman named Brown'.[1]

Garrick said of him: 'Such a villain sure never existed: his scheme is now abuse', and wrote on him the epigram

> 'For physic and farces his equal there scarce is,
> His farces are physic, his physic a farce is.'

Fielding writes of him 'this *hill* was only a little paltry *dunghill*... long levelled with the dirt'. Speaking of Hill and of Orator Henley together, Isaac Disraeli has observed: 'Never two authors were more constantly pelted with epigrams, or buffeted in literary quarrels.'[2] Prints also appeared in ridicule of his cowardice, after his drubbing by Brown, in one of which a number of doctors stand round his bed, while one of them cries 'Sell your sword, it is only an incumbrance'. Thus Burke is entering into one of the more notorious scrimmages of the eighteenth-century literary world in this little *jeu d'esprit* on 'the Inspector', of whom Smart wrote—to quote again from *The Hilliad*—

> 'Yet strange variety shall check thy life—
> Thou grand dictator of each public show,
> Wit, moralist, quack, harlequin and beau.'

[1] *D.N.B.*

[2] See Isaac Disraeli, *Calamities and Quarrels of Authors, edited by his son the Earl of Beaconsfield* (1881), p. 363.

# A FUNERAL ORATION ON THE INSPECTOR* TO BE PRONOUNCED IN THE BEDFORD COFFEE HOUSE BY MR MACKLIN.† BY E.B.

LONDON                                                                1751

Since the Inspector is now no more, Since he can no longer pay the usual Tribute of Praise to his own Merit, it becomes the Duty of all who were his rivals in the admiration of that Merit to deplore the fatal Loss of it, and to Continue a panegyric on their side which nothing but Death could interrupt on his. Even in Death itself it was his pleasing theme, the ruling Passion of his Life, dictated his dying Words; and in his last moments he could parallel himself with none but—Caesar—*Ne non procumbat honeste.*

Could we stretch our View further we might see our Narcissus contemplating in the stygian water, that dear, that self-applauded form. Let us leave him to the happy Contemplation of what he is; Let us turn òur eyes to what he was. And here, it is hard to know where to begin or when to end. His perfections were like a Circle, Compleat in themselves, and everywhere equal. Nay more, they were all his own. He has imitated nobody, and nobody, we dare venture to affirm, will ever imitate him. Great Genius[es] never compass their Ends by ordinary Methods. The Inspector, a man born to illustrate all good Maxims, has illustrated this. What an uncommon Genius must he have had, who took his way to admiration by the road

* Dr Hill, writer of a paper so named.
† There were several remarkably impudent fellows on the Town, but this Gentleman, a Comedian, outfaced them all. [(Note in the M.S.) Macklin (1697?–1797) was an actor and dramatist. 'Between 1748 and 1750 Macklin was in Dublin, where he and his wife were engaged by Sheridan at £800 a year. On leaving Dublin Macklin migrated to Covent Garden' (*D.N.B.*).]

42

which leads Directly to Contempt; who Established an opinion of his Modesty by self-adoration, of his courage by suffering, of his religion by Gallantry, of his Gallantry by his Saturday's Papers,* and of his Consistency by all?

This behaviour may to the Vulgar have seemed Unaccountable. You, Gentlemen, can look further than the outside. You have seen him in his most conspicuous Scenes; and therefore I chuse you for my Audience, because you can Supply by your Memory the defects of my Elocution. And Why should we hesitate to do Justice to him, who has always done it to the World? Has he ever spoken ill of any Body, to whom he has not given Occasion to speak worse of him? But if we admire his Justice, what Encomiums will suit his prudence in that admirable distinction which he Establish'd between the Inspector and Doctor Hill; a Distinction so Slippery that no knot could hold him. If the inspector was a libeller, Doctor Hill was, notwithstanding, a good natured man. If the Inspector proposed Marriage, Doctor Hill slipt out of the Noose. On the other hand, if Doctor Hill was a man of profess'd Bravery, the Inspector might have been conscientious in Duelling. If Doctor Hill suffered a Publick Threshing, The Inspector felt no hurt in body or Reputation. The Old Stoic could never say with more constancy 'vent your fury on this trunk, you can never hurt me'. This Admirable Lesson of Subterfuge he learn'd (where he learn'd many other good Lessons) from those Beasts who contrive two holes, that, if they are attacked in one, they may escape thro' the other, or rather from those Excellent Moral Entertainments the Pantomimes, wherein, when everybody thinks Harlequin fast, he appears when nobody Expected him.

It is hard to Sustain one Character well. He has done more; he has Sustained two.—Two such as could separately have graced the most eminent persons; two such as none could have thought Compatible in one. He has held them in all things.

* The saturday papers were always on Religious Subjects.

At Ranelagh he was a Coxecomb, at home he was a Philosopher. At Ranelagh he endured a drubbing, at home he and Major England gave one.

Should we rest on one of his virtues, it would disable us from giving his others their due. Should we attempt to praise all, we could give its proper honours to None. What shall we say? Where to fix?—Chance not Choice must direct us. He was such a Lover of Literature that he wo'd not accept an ill Spelt Challenge; such an Enemy to foppery that, for it, he Libell'd a man he own'd he never saw; So humble that he descended to Lie; so patient that he Endured a Drubbing, so Courageous that he Hectored after it. What a more sign of true Bravery and fertile invention that to Multiply one man into fifteen? What of a sober and Correct judgment than to diminish them afterwards to ten, to six, to four?—Death, the Cruel hand of Death, cut him short reducing them to one. It was the practice of Virgil, in the morning to write a vast Number of rude lines, and to spend the day in reducing them. This he called licking the Bear.[1] Thus the Inspector, in his rage of Invention, rais'd a monstrous Story, then Licked it into Shape and Probability.

I am myself, as you all know, a player; and, without Vanity, a pretty good one. Yet notwithstanding my Partiality to the stage, I can by no means endure a Comparison I have[2] generally made between our Hero and Falstaff. Falstaff fell as much below the Inspector in Merit as he Exceeded him in Bulk. He began in a probable story and ended in a gross one. The Inspector began ill, but has Constantly mended. In one thing, indeed, they are both Equally admirable—at a subterfuge. Both excellent at Brazening out a Drubbing.

Gentlemen, such were the virtues that adorn'd his Life. His

---

[1] 'Non absurde carmen se more ursae parere dicens et lambendo demum effingere' (Suetonius, *Life of Vergil*). 'Wittily saying that he produced a poem and in the manner of a she-bear licked it into shape.'

[2] Read 'hear'?

Death was the Proper close of such a scene. The King of Silence let fall the Curtain amid the applause of all the Spectators. I have seen Othello fall, Hamlet slain, Caesar butchered. These have I seen unmov'd. I have personated Iago, I have acted the Jew. Yet here, and here alone, have I been forced to shed tears, true unfeigned, untheatrical tears. Dixi.

(*Cetera desunt.* From here we have mere notes.)
Never had man *such* funeral Applause.

the Revenge.

Thee shall each Ale-house, thee each gill house mourn
And—

Dunciad.

## [ 8 ]

This piece has little interest except as illustrating one aspect of Burke's course of study.

❧

# A PLAN FOR ARGUING
# BY EDMUND BURKE

Arguments are used to convince us, (1) of some natural truth—(2) To establish some Matter of fact—or (3) to persuade us to do something.

1. Arguments concerning the Nature of any being can only be taken from the Investigation of its Properties and the Analogy they bear to each other.

2. The Credibility of Matter of fact is made out, 1st, by considering its Probability with Regard to General Experience.

2ndly, by its Agreement with the particular circumstances of time, place, manners, Customs etc.

3rdly, by the Credit of the Relator, which is founded 1st. on his Impartiality, 2nd. on his Consistency with himself, 3rd. with others, 4th. on his being a Competent Judge of the Matter of fact, 5th. on his having sufficient means of being informed, 6th. on his being credulous or incredulous. If any of these, or many, are wanting, so is the fact more or less credible.

3. The Arguments that persuade to any Resolution are taken either 1st. from Justice, 2nd. from Interest or 3rd. from Affection.

1st. from *Justice*, that it suits 1st. the Law of God, 2nd. the general Notion of Virtue, 3rd. the Laws of the land or 4th. the Law of Opinion.

2nd. The Arguments to be drawn *from Interest* are very extensive as they consist in such different Relations and vary so much with Circumstances. However I shall venture to throw them under two heads,

1st the present advantages, 2nd the Consequences.

1. If any thing is to be deliberated, we ask is it necessary at all? Is it so at this time? In this Manner? What Mischief will it prevent, or what good will it produce? Will it not cause as great an Evil as is meant to be remedied? Is it the best? Will it give anybody offence? Will it advance our credit, our Strength, our Riches? Is it compatible with other Resolutions, or will it discompose the order and regularity of anything more Essential? How have others acted in the like Case? Will it be suitable to our Circumstances? Are we well able to do it?

2. What will be the Consequences? Will our want of success involve us or our friends or partizans in any perplexity? Tho' it should serve in the present emergency, may it not hurt by being continued, by being applied to what it was not originally intended for? Can it introduce any bad habit, or be of ill Example, or *e contra* of all these? Or may our Enemies derive any immediate or any future advantage to their own profit or credit, or to our discredit?

3rd. *from Affection*, all such arguments are drawn from the passions, or from Authority. To invent Arguments without a thorough knowledge of the Subject is clearly impossible. But the Art of Invention does two things—

1. It suggests to us more readily those Parts of our actual knowledge which may help towards illustrating the matter before us, and

2. It suggests to us those heads of Examination which may lead, if pursued with effect, into a knowledge of the Subject.

So that the Art of Invention may properly be considered as the method of calling up what we do know and investigating that of which we are ignorant.

Let us pass over whatever regards Speculation, and only consider this point in those things which belong to Civil Life; which chiefly resolve themselves into the Deliberative, whether certain things are fit to be done or forborne upon the Principles of Justice on the one hand—and of Convenience on the other.

On the head of Justice it is fit to ask—

Whether, the thing is capable of Right, viz Propriety.

Who has the right? how it is capable of right?

Whence has he it?

What are its Limits?

How long has it subsisted?

What infringements have been made?

What opinions have been formed on it?

Are they weighty, numerous, popular?

Is there any admittance of an Adversary?

What is the name of the thing and the Right, and whence is that name derived?

What is it like—or unlike?

 In its substance ⎫
 In its reason  ⎬
 In its use   ⎭

Now as to Convenience—

 Is the thing necessary?

  Whence does the Necessity arise? ⎫
  How have we done before?  ⎬
  Are there no other Expedients? ⎭

Is it necessary at this time?
  In this manner?
  In this Extent?
Is it expedient, near, remote, certain, or contingent?
  does it unsettle nothing else?
  does it introduce any Evil or Good?
  does it agree with other parts of a System?
  Will it offend or please?
  Will it fall in with, or contradict, opinion?
  the Consequence, if we omit it, simply, or drop, after
    having begun it?
  Is the thing difficult or easy—time,
                         Manner,
                         our strength,
                         opposite.
  How may the Difficulty be overcome?—
                         by Perseverance?
                         calling help? what help?
                         taking new method?
                         persuing the former?
  What is against us—is it so much as thought?[1]
  What ballances?
  What have others done in our Circumstances?
  What opinions have been about it?
  I think something in the way of Categories of great
  Use—They are, 1 Substantia, 2 Quantitas, 3 Qualitas,
  4 Relatio, 5 Actio, 5 Passio, 7 Ubi, 8 Quando, 9 Situs,
  10 habitus—these serve to class our Ideas—
Now as to the thing to be done—besides simple Justice and
Convenience, there are several heads of Argument—will it be
[to] our Credit, will it shew Courage, firmness, Wisdom—or the
Contrary? Is it approved of us? Is it consistent or contrary to
our Character?

          [1] I.e. as it is thought to be?

Will it serve to supply the want of something else?
Is it likely to be forwarded or retarded by the persons ingaged?
Now all Personalities[1] are Praise, Blame or Excuse.

With regard to Praise} Virtue, has a  Correspondent Vice
⎰ *e contra.*

Capacity, one capacity implies or
excludes another.

fortune, to be relied upon *e contra.*

## [ 9 ]

The following skit has reference to Sir James Lowther, Bart., who
died in 1755, and is described in the *Gentleman's Magazine* as
'reckoned the richest commoner in Great Britain, and worth about
a million'. It is interesting to note that his estate of Whitehaven and
about £2,000,000 passed on his death to his cousin, another Sir
James Lowther—of Maude Meaburn—who later became 1st Earl
of Lonsdale, and appears also to have been of a miserly character,
and who by borrowing some thousands of pounds from his agent,
William Wordsworth's father, and never repaying it, affected ad-
versely the fortunes of the poet himself until 1802, when his heir
repaid the money.

∾

# A LETTER TO SIR JAMES LOWTHER
# A MOST NOTORIOUS MISER WHO
# SPENT ABOUT £300 A YEAR OUT
# OF £30,000 A YEAR

MAY 1752

## [By Edmund Burke]

Sir,

I have not the Honour of being Personally known to you,
but I am so well acquainted with your Character, that I am

---

[1] Or 'Pasonalties'. The word is scarcely legible, and certainly not
intelligible.

convinced I cannot apply to any person in my necessities so properly as to Sir James Lowther. The World allows you to have as great a Share of understanding as fortune; you cannot Object to a reasonable request because it is an uncommon one; and when you have nothing to object on the side of reason, certainly you can have no impediment on the side of Riches. I desire you to lend me one hundred pounds without bond or any other security. This demand some will think extremely modest. Others (among whom I fear I must reckon yourself) will think me the most impudent man alive for it. I will allow this; but then you must allow me to insist on this as the strongest argument for your granting my request, and the strongest proof of my future gratitude for that favour. Had you given it to a modest man, he would Blush to lye under an obligation, and to save his own Credit would detract from yours. But I shall proclaim it to the world; not a jot of the Glory of the Action shall be lost; for as I was not ashamed to ask this favour, I will not hesitate publickly to acknowledge it. Perhaps sir, you think, there is little honour to be had from Actions of this nature. I believe you think justly. Here again my impudence may be of Service; it will enable me with great Assurance to Assert that you gave an hundred pounds more than I ask'd; and then no man alive will believe I received a farthing. If you comply with this request, you will do me infinite Service;— pardon me, if I Say you will do yourself no less. First it will deliver me from want. What misery, Anxiety, shame and Torment are contained in that word, I need not explain to you, sir, who are so sensible to this that you have made it the whole study of a Long and Laborious Life to avoid the least possibility of this evil. You will serve yourself, and what you seem to regard much more, you will not hurt your heir. Can he in Spending, or can you in saving, feel the Loss of such a trifle? It will certainly even add length of Days to you; so that you may live to save yet more. So much as you take from your fortune so much do you take from that Gentleman's daily Prayers for your Death; and so much do you add to mine for your Preservation. See then, sir, the Difference, and judge which you ought to favour. Your heir cannot suffer in the least by this Gift; I shall be undone without it. He prays for your Death, that he may get all you have; I pray for your Life;— as well for what I have got, as for the hope of getting still more. Our interests are closely united; but yours and his are utterly incompatible. You see I own freely I am guided by my Interest; but sure, you must think very meanly of my understanding if I fail'd to pay a due regard to so material a point. If my interest did not prompt to desire your acquaintance, my inclination would force me to it. I have long had a great Esteem for your Character. If Similitude of manners be a foundation of friendship, none can bid fairer for it than we do. The World says you love money; if I were of Consequence Enough it would Say the same of me. In what then do we differ? In this only;—you enjoy your Desires; I still languish; you are worth a Million, I am not master of a Single Groat. How easy were it for you to make our resemblance, and consequently our friendship, quite Compleat? You may object that my want of money is proof that I don't love it as I ought; I might answer that I am an unpossessing lover, ten times more amorous, more passionate, more eager, than he that enjoys the height of all his wishes. But I won't play the hypocrite; I won't compare myself to you. Perhaps I don't value riches sufficiently; 'tis a fault common to youth; but it is such a one as I shall every day mend of. I have not yet had much money and must be excused if I don't set a right Value on it. For the value encreases with possession; as I observe from your Conduct, and that of some other wise men whose Conduct I would be proud to imitate. You have no Children; and you need not lament that you had none, if your Children might only be known to belong to you by squandering what you have amassed. But give me an hundred pounds; I shall take your Example with your money. I will save, I will hoard, I will scrape, I will scramble, I will starve. Everybody shall Cry there goes a *Lowther*. I will represent you better than an hundred sons. Let me end this Long Letter. If you approve my scheme, Let me have an hundred pounds with your advice how to use it. That will make me a fortune, and a fortune will make me happy. If you are displeased, punish me, Sir; give me an hundred pounds and leave me to my own Discretion in using it. It will plunge me into new Distresses and I shall be ruined. Take which course you will, and you will not fail to oblige.

Your very faithfull    E. B.

## [ 10 ]

This sketch of the character of Jane Nugent, Burke's future wife, has been highly praised by Prior in his *Life of Burke*, and has certainly great charm.

Prior calls it 'the idea of a perfect wife. . . which he presented to her one morning on the anniversary of their marriage'. But the concluding paragraph, which Prior omits—'Who can see and know such a Creature and not love to Distraction? Who can know her, and himself, and entertain much hope?'—would seem to indicate that it was written before his marriage. Though it is possible that Burke may not have shown it to his wife until 'the anniversary of his marriage', omitting, as Prior has done, the rather touching final paragraph.

∾

# THE CHARACTER OF — [MRS EDMUND BURKE]

### [By Edmund Burke]

I intend to give my Idea of a woman. If it at all answers any Original I shall be pleased; for if such a person really exists as

52

I would describe, she must be far Superior to any Description, and such as I must love too well to be able to paint as I ought.

She is handsome; but it is a Beauty not arising from features, from Complexion and Shape. She has all these in an high degree; but whoever looks at her never perceives them, nor makes them the Topic of his Praise. 'Tis all the sweetness of Temper, Benevolence, Innocence and Sensibility which a face can express, that forms her beauty.

She has a face that just raises your attention at first sight; it grows on you every moment, and you wonder it did no more than raise your Attention at first.

Her Eyes have a mild light, but they awe you when she pleases; they command like a good man out of office, not by Authority but virtue.

Her features are not perfectly regular; this Sort of Exactness is more to be praised than loved; it is never animated.

Her stature is not tall. She is not to be the admiration of everybody, but the happiness of one.

She has all the Delicacy that does not Exclude firmness.

She has all the Softness that does not imply weakness.

There is often more of the Coquet shewn in an Effected plainness, than a Tawdry finery; she is always clean without preciseness or affectation.

Her Gravity is a gentle thoughtfulness that Softens the features without discomposing them. She is usually grave.

Her Smiles are . . . inexpressible—

Her Voice is a low, Soft musick; not formed to rule in publick Assemblies, but to charm those who can distinguish a Company from a Croud. It has this advantage, you must come Close to her to hear it.

To describe her body, describes her mind; one is the Transcript of the other.

Her understanding is not shewn in the Variety of matters it exerts itself on, but the goodness of the Choice she makes.

She does not Shew it so much in doing or Saying striking things, as in avoiding such as she ought not to say or do.

She discovers the right from the wrong in things not by reasoning, but Sagacity.

Most women, and many good ones, have a Closeness and something Selfish in their Disposition:—She has a true generosity of Temper. The most extravagant cannot be more willing to give; the most Covetous not more cautious to whom they give.

No person of so few years can know the world better: no person was ever less corrupted by that knowledge. Her politeness seems to flow rather from a natural disposition to oblige, than from any rules on that subject; and therefore never fails to Strike those who understand good breeding, and those who do not.

She does not run with a Girlish eagerness into new freindships; which as they have no foundation in reason, only tend to multiply and imbitter[1] disputes. 'Tis long before she chuses; but then it is fixid forever; and the first hours of romantick friendships are not more warm than hers after years.

As she never disgraces her good nature by severe reflections on any body, so she never degrades her Judgement by immoderate or ill-placed praises; for everything violent is contrary to the Gentleness of her disposition, and the evenness of her virtue. She has a steady and firm mind, which takes no more from the female Character than the Solidity of marble does from its Polish and Lustre.

She has such virtues as make us value the truely great of our own Sex. She has all the winning Graces that make us love even the faults we see in the weak and Beautiful of hers.

Who can see and know such a Creature and not love to Distraction?

Who can know her, and himself, and entertain much hope?

E.B.

---

[1] The MS. rendering.

WILLIAM BURKE, by Reynolds

It is not revealed at what period William Burke wrote this Character
of Mrs Edmund Burke.

❧

## A CHARACTER OF THE SAME
## LADY DRAWN BY A FRIEND

[By William Burke]

Most women are so governed by Custom, that their own hearts
have little to do with their Conduct; they have nothing of their
own. Are they wrong, or are they right, 'tis not them but
Custom we ought to condemn or admire. But with Amata 'tis
far otherwise;—her heart directs her in every step she takes, and
all that softness of manners, that sweetness of Behaviour that
binds us so to Amata, are owing to the goodness of her heart.
Her worth is all owing to herself;—Custom can have no share
in what we praise. On the other hand were she in any point not
right, the world must bear no part of the Blame; it must all lie
on her own Shoulders. But the load is so light, that, delicate as
those lovely Shoulders are, she may easily bear it.

However just the Charge may be that women love talk,
Amata certainly is no talker; for the Company of her own sex,
perhaps a little too silent. But if the presence of men of Sense,
at any time leads the Conversation to such serious Topicks as
most women think exclude them the Company, as Effectually
as if a Strange Language were spoken, 'tis then Amata in her
silence gives proof of her prudence and good Sense. For 'tis
such an attentive Silence as apparently shows her to be still one
of the Company. And indeed I have sometimes known this
attention so enable her with a certain sagacity to give lights in
points wherein the very Persons she attended to were in the

Dark, that she has Charmed and informed them to whom she listened for information. No wonder, then, if men of Sense are happy in the Company of Amata, nor is it more wonder that she is not fond of the tittle tattle of her own Sex. Indeed nobody is more above their little fears, Triflings and Irresolutions than Amata. She, however pretty some Ladies might think it, would be ashamed to Change her opinions with the moments. There is a Steddiness in her heart, that is worthy of her Character, and is a real virtue. But virtues themselves have their places: Amata sometimes is perhaps too fixt on trifling occasions; and I fear we may not call that steddiness or resolution: the ill-natured would call it *Stubbornness*; and the very friends of Amata would find it difficult to show them they were mistaken. But dare I own this and name Amata, when I have allowed that the world must not share in any the least Title if Amata were to blame? Yes; I dare! For her very faults, you see, are but virtues in Extreams: and to say the Truth, I would not wish to see her break her resolution when once made. But I would advise her not to take any resolution at all on trifling occasions.

But do I pretend to advise? I have seen her yeild up her opinion and quit her intention at some times with such a sweet engaging sweetness, that I could swear no Creature on Earth can be free[er] from stubbornness than Amata.

I wish I could as easily acquit her of a little Idleness, that has some how crept upon her; and which is the more dangerous as it has escaped herself, at the very time that it occasions some little (Actions, I cannot Say but some) omissions rather, that ought not to be Left undone by Amata. In others they might be pardonable; but in her we forgive nothing. I wish she would examine herself. Her own heart must convince her, of what no friend can. For what friend can be so attentive to his own Arguments, or even to her welfare, as to help looking on the most engaging face in the world? And the moment he does that, his eyes will betray his reason. For who that looks on the lovely Amata can longer suppose she has one single fault? I'm sure there lives not one, of whom this might be more freely thought than of Amata.

She is indeed the loveliest, and best of human Creatures; but still she is, and her unfeigned piety shows us she knows herself to *be*, an Human Creature.

## [ 12 ]

This piece is a Character of William Burke by Edmund.

As Dixon Wecter has observed, 'In view of the intimate role which William Burke was to play in his kinsman's affairs...this sketch called "Phidippus" is of considerable interest' (*Edmund Burke and his Kinsmen*, p. 10).

∽

## THE CHARACTER OF PHIDIPPUS

### [By Edmund Burke]

Though at first View it may appear otherwise, the last degree of intimacy with any person is not a very favourable Circumstance to him who draws his Character. Too great a Variety of things present themselves to us at once, and we are oppressed by this abundance; we grow too attentive to every little line and stroke in the Countenance, to hit off a general likeness happily. There is no man whom I know more interiorly than Phidippus, I know his Virtues and love them, but this does not hinder me from observing upon his Defects, I am not blinded with love, neither do I squint from Malice.

Phidippus has a mind endued with the most quick poi[g]nant and delicate feelings that I ever knew. Love, Grief, Joy, hatred, are with him sudden and Violent. They come on like fits; nothing can oppose them whilst they last; and they tear up his Soul from the very bottom. These fits at the time when you think them most Violent, easily pass away. They leave him in a Serenity w$^{ch}$ has not the least remain of the former passions; these, notwithstanding, after some time appear again with all their former Violence, commit their former Havoc, and pass away with the former facility. His passions are not Gales nor storms; but a sort of Sudden Gusts preceded and followed by the profoundest Calm.

The heart of Phidippus has a tenderness even to the feminine; a facility w$^{ch}$ the address in those whom he loves may manage; but this is accompanied with a kind of suspicion, a sort of Turn of Stomach which when it is raised nothing can allay. His mind in this respect is like the Down of fouls;—whilst you stroke them with the grain nothing can be more smooth; if you rub against it, nothing more rough and unpliable.

He has a very exquisite Taste and it is that Taste that governs him. I do not mean solely a Taste for Books, but a Taste in men, in actions, in life. The least false Ornament in the one, the least false Pretence or affectation in the other disgusts, wounds him. But, as exquisite feeling and pain are Closely allied, and it is the nature of Such feeling to be apprehensive of pain from whatever approaches it, he has a sort of Suspicion— that everything which appears strong has a false appearance. He therefore sets himself violently against it; and thus very often a prejudice arising from a quick feeling takes away the accuracy of Judgement that otherwise that Sharp perception might procure.

This observed is a key to a great part of his Character and conduct. His Judgements upon books are uncommonly exact and true; but this judgement in general does not extend to any Books but those who [*sic*] have something elegant in their Subject and matter, or some acuteness in the thoughts or style. Other Matters he does not like; neither does he form any Judgement on them to be depended upon.

The understanding of Phidippus is strong and Quick but it is not Steady. He looks at many things like a man who Stand[s] in a boat. He sees them in their proper colours, he sees them plainly; but he does not always keep them long enough in his Eye in the same posture to make the most useful Judgement on them. If he catches the Object in a happy moment, his Judgement is of the very best kind, and has all those graces which attend what is called *an happiness.* If he misses this, he does not easily recover it.

Therefore employ Phidippus where a penetration into the Character of mankind is necessary, where an opportunity never to be retrieved is to be laid hold on; where a happy turn of the Affair determines its fate;—not where attention, care, and power of comparing various and discordant matters, to reconcile them, are required.

Phidippus would make an excellent ambassador.

Phidippus without being tall or elegant in his person, has the aspect of a Gentleman; without excelling in any polite Exercise has the Demeanour of that character; without being perfectly easy, he has a Delicacy in his behaviour that looks like Ease, and pleases perhaps more than ease itself, by its not being uniform.

You would take Phidippus for a man confident and assuming; but in reallity he has nothing less in his Character. He is timorous and diffident; he has a quick sense of the least disgrace. If you see Phidippus positive and violent, do not think I am wrong in my observation. This violence is only a sort of Clamour in which he would drown his own fears.

## [ 13 ]

This piece is in William Burke's handwriting; but one or two passages in it are similar to portions of pieces definitely assigned to Edmund (see Introduction, p. 6). It is very probable, therefore, that this also is by him.

◌

## THE WAY TO PREFERMENT

[Most probably by Edmund Burke]

No Man scarce is possessed of any distinguishing Quality who is not fond of displaying that mark of Distinction on All occasions.

I never yet had a quarter of an hour's conversation with a stranger, before I knew whether he had a fortune or not. I always take a Man's silence on that head as an implicit acknowledgement of his Poverty. A Great Genius discovers himself in a Moment; and you cannot address yourself to any [such] Man, without his letting you know what an extraordinary person you have the honour to converse with;[1] whether he values himself for Criticism or Poetry, whether he be a Person of profound Learning, or whether he has an Ingenious and elegant contempt for all learning. But whatever Satisfaction this Display may afford a Man's Vanity, Experience shews it has the worst effects on his Interest. It is a false Notion that Abilities have ever recommended a Man to the good Offices of any; and tho' much Care has been expended, and much advice given, concerning setting off our Parts to the best advantage, I think

[1] 'Burke, sir, is such a man, that if you met him for the first time in the street, when you were stopped by a drove of oxen, and you stepped aside to take shelter but for five minutes, he'd talk to you in such a manner, that, when you parted, you would say This is an extraordinary man.' Boswell's *Life of Johnson* (Croker, 1844), vol. IV, p. 23.

the great Art is that of concealing one's Parts to the best advantage. 'Tis a pity we have so little written on so good a Subject, and one so fit to set forth the Capacity of the Author. It was formerly a matter of wonder to me when I saw men who had neither Wit to entertain, Judgement to instruct, Abilities to serve, nor any one Qualification whatsoever to recommend them to the Notice of the world, rise from fortunes as contemptible as their Characters, to the highest Offices and the greatest Possessions, without the wonder of almost anybody; or any enquiry into the Causes of this extraordinary fortune. Only some of the shrewder sort would observe 'that he was a clever fellow and played his Cards well'.

I own this used to give me some uneasiness, and not a few reflexions. You will call them envious ones;—how much better I deserved all this myself, and took comfort that *my* parts, *my* intrinsic Merit, were a much better possession than his Equipage;[1] tho' I confess, even in my own Eyes, my own Merit made but a poor figure when the said Equipage made its Appearance.

In the intervals of Spleen I used to examine what latent Qualities made amends for the Apparent Want of Merit in such Persons. But after much thinking, I am convinced their Rise was owing to this very want of Merit and nothing else. I was satisfied that to conceal a Man's talent was the way to make it useful to him; and that none could so happily conceal it as he that had nothing to shew. I have no doubt of the truth of these remarks. The foundations on which they are built may perhaps not be so satisfactory. But they are grounded on certain observations taken from human Nature;—the first is—that almost every man, however problematical it may appear to others, takes himself for a little God. If he be a great Man, then he is a Deity Majorum Gentium. And so from the highest to the lowest.

[1] Cf. above, no. 6, ll. 70–4 and my Introduction, p. 7, on this, no. 13.

In consequence of this Creed, any Man who takes on himself any such attributes, manifestly affronts this God; and can therefore never be loved or advanced by him, tho' he should employ these very attributes in his Service. The person whom he has in the highest Contempt has the first Place in his Affections. An utter Annihilation is the way to become considerable; and hence has arisen that emphatical Phraise about Courts '*his Creature*'. The less this being has of his own, either in Body or Soul, understanding or Will, the more completely he belongs to his Creator. the more he is loved by him, and the fitter to make another being well known by the name of — among the Vulgar; tho' among the Gods he is called —, in which Character he serves so well, that at last he gets off his state of Instrumentality and becomes a working cause himself.

Of all sort of flattery, Men delight most in that Species called the Demonstrative. Any Person can tell him 'You are superior to all Mankind'; but he does more, that shows you, past doubt, you are Superior to himself. Men of Wit can flatter; but, in the very Act, half, and more than half, the Credit falls on the flatterer for doing it so ingeniously. These hints are to make Men of no Talents contented with their lot; and others not so fond of showing their's—My own Case.

Most families intimate with some below them.

Excuses for not serving Men of Merit.[1]

---

[1] These two sentences are written very small, as memoranda (?), in the MS.

This piece, as is noticed in the Introduction (p. 7 above), bears a close resemblance to one of Burke's essays in *The Reformer*. The passage beginning 'if you ask a conventicler...' (p. 64, l. 13), also, is clearly related to a passage in no. 19: 'To instance in the Methodist:—all their terms...are chosen by them too unintelligible and inexplicable, for fear the Understanding should have any play.... When a reason of their faith is demanded, this cant is the answer you receive...' (p. 97 below).

◆

# *THE MAN OF SPIRIT*

## [By Edmund Burke]

There are men who pass for great Spirits by neglecting or trampling upon all the Decent Regulations of living, conversing, and writing. Their Admirers see all their faults, and are ready enough to confess them, but it is the Misfortune of Men of Genius to be excentric and extravagant.[1] There is nothing so monstrous which this Character of Genius will not excuse. Nay people go further and make their very weaknesses and follies pass for convincing proofs of their Superior Talents. They have got a reverse way of judging of Men's Capacities, not by what they have, but by what they have not. I have often been at a loss to find a Criterion of Genius in such cases. Having examined what seemed to me to constitute Parts and an agreable and proper use of them, I found to my Surprise that none of these were in the least concerned in the formation of a Genius. If I ask whether this Person of Genius be really a Man of sound Judgement, I am told he has too much fire to be very Judicious. If I enquire into the strength of his Memory, I am

[1] I.e. their admirers say it is.

laughed at for supposing a Man of Wit can have any. If I ask about his learning, he is a natural Genius. Our man of Genius is very stupid and uninstructive in company; but then he is all for the Closet.[1] If I enquire of his writings, 'tis ten to one but I hear he is too impatient to finish anything. If I am fortunate enough to light on some of his works, it is in vain that I mention a thousand objections to them. Every fault I mention serves to establish his Character;—for Men of Genius are never correct. This Humour of substituting something equivocal in the Place of real Merit, and, having once supposed that, to believe all the rest to be not only useless but a sort of Proof that he wants that something, is very common among ordinary Understandings. If you ask a conventicler about the Abilities of his Preacher he tells you he is a most wonderful Man. Has he a good Method? No: No method at all. Are his Arguments cogent and clear? He uses no Arguments;—that would savour of human Wisdom. But is his Language elegant? No, all that is vanity! Where then is his Excellence? He has the Spirit.

A sort of fellow that is rough and Brutish in his manners, dissolute in his Life, extravagant in his opinions, that is arrogant, contentious, and careless of his own Interest, thankless for what he has received, inconstant, one, while caressing, the next Moment abusing the same Man, without any sort of human Affection—This is a Character which imposes upon a great Many honest, and even some knowing, Persons for a Man of Genius. And all those who flourish in the Opinion of the town at present, and whom I have had the happiness of seeing are just of that Character. 'Tis a Pity he is such a Person; yet if [he] were not, he would lose all his Admirers. When once the Character is assumed, he is dispensed with observing any forms. Half his time he is Gloomy, sullen and dejected for Men of Wit are always in the Vapours;—and the other half,

[1] I.e. so his admirers say.

outrageously *boisterous* not merry. His only proof of Good Nature is that he is negligent of his own Affairs.

I have often observed a Parcel of turkeys stunning one with the strange Noise they make; and it represented to me the Clamours of our House of common[s] Patriots. And the Image was still strengthened when the Hen-wife came out and threw a little pollard[1] among them. They were before heckling in a prodigiously loud Concert; their feathers were all ruf[f]led and every bird seemed to chal[l]enge you. But no sooner had the hen-wife's bounteous hand thrown the pollard down, than every Mouth was silent, every feather was quite Smooth; and if now there was any Contention, it was only who should get the Pollard.

## [ 15 ]

This piece is almost certainly by Edmund Burke (see Introduction, p. 7).

∽

## *A TRUE GENIUS*

[Almost certainly by Edmund Burke]

As a great Genius is but rarely found, so is he but rarely of any Use, never but on Extraordinary Occasions and great Emergencies. At other times it is often hurtful, those are then wanted who lye in an ordinary road.

A Genius suffers in most Cases except where it is to work all of itself, and where fortune has no Place. There it can only be seen indisputably.

That may be called a Genius which compasses great things by the Exertion of some great faculty of the Mind in a new and striking bold Manner. One Great Action is not a sufficient

---

[1] 'Bran sifted from flour' (*Oxford English Dictionary*).

proof of such a Genius. The Reduction of Rochelle alone would not have eternized Richlieu in the Roll of Great Genius. There must be a Series in their Actions; and all proceeding from the same Spirit and Influence.

Many Generals know how to fight, and have the fortune to conquer too; but 'tis the Part of a Great Genius to form a bold and surprising Plan full of Difficulties, such as astonish and seem unaccountable to an ordinary Spirit; and yet such as shew[1] by their effects, they were the best that could be chosen. A Man who proceeds in the ordinary Method proceeds like a Machine: We know what to oppose to every Motion; we see all his Scheme: We can be sure what Step he will take next, and it is our own fault if he has any success: But a true Genius aims at his Point by such Methods as leave us in the dark for his Design, till we see and feel the Execution.

He seems to hazard everything;—and striking at the heart of the Matter, neglects all the inferior Parts. Scipio, when Annibal was in the midst of Italy, at the head of his Victorious troops, leaves Italy undefended; and marches his Army directly to Carthage.

This was a great plan; and not inferiour to Hannibal's astonishing March from Afric thro Spain and Gaul over the Apennine[s] and Alps into Italy.

And to mention a no less example of latter Ages, the Duke of Parma, to support the Spanish Interest in France, quits all his Conquest in the low Countries, and all his prospects of more,—pendent opera interrupta, minaeq[ue] murorum ingentes aequataque machina Coelo.[2]

---

[1] To be grammatical this should read, 'shews by its (the plan's) effects, it was the best. . .'.

[2] The interrupted works are held up,—the huge threatenings of walls and the machine high as the Heaven (Virgil, *Aeneid*, IV, 88–9).

This piece is almost certainly by Edmund Burke. It is apparently in his handwriting, and it contains several passages very typical of his thought: for example, 'enthusiasm is a sort of Instinct, in those who possess it, that operates, like all Instincts, better than a mean Species of Reason' (see also Introduction, p. 8).

✿

## RELIGION OF NO EFFICACY CON-SIDERED AS A STATE ENGINE

[Almost certainly by Edmund Burke]

Nothing can operate but from its own principles. The Principle of Religion is that God attends to our actions to reward and punish them. This Principle has an independent Operation, and Influences our Actions much to the Benefit of civil Society. But then the Influence on civil Society is only an oblique Influence. The Direct Influence is the civil Law itself, its own Principles and its own Sanctions. If you attempt to make the end of Religion to be its Utility to human Society, to make it only a sort of supplement to the Law, and insist principally upon this Topic, as is very common to do, you then change its principle of Operation, which consists on Views beyond this Life, to a consideration of another kind, and of an inferiour kind; and thus, by forcing it against its Nature to become a Political Engine, You make it an Engine of no efficacy at all. It can never operate for the Benefit of human Society but when we think it is directed quite another way: because it then only operates from its own principle. Will any Man believe that eternal rewards and Punishments are the Sanctions of Momentary things of no Concern? Will he not think it a strange Machine that employs so vast, so immense a force, such a grand Apparatus to move so insignificant a weight? Is it not much more natural, much more in the order of things, to suppose that if a reasonable Creature is to determine of his own Destiny so as to determine him for Bliss or for Misery everlastingly, that the Trial is made subservient to a great End of the last Importance, and that Trial the *Means* of Attaining that End, rather than that all Eternity should be subservient to the purposes of a moment? When we are told this,[1] we cool immediately. The Springs are seen; we value ourselves on the Discovery; we cast Religion to the Vulgar and lose all restraint. For as we confine the Ends of Religion to this world, we naturally annihilate its Operation, which must wholly depend upon the Consideration of another. Men never gain anything, by forcing Nature to conform to their Politicks. I know the Clergy, shamed and frightend at the Imputation of Enthusiasm, endeavour to cover Religion under the Shield of Reason, which will have some force with their Adversaries. But God has been pleased to give Mankind an Enthusiasm to supply the want of Reason; and truely, Enthusiasm comes nearer the great and comprehensive Reason in its effects, though not in the Manner of Operation, than the Common Reason does; which works on confined, narrow, common, and therefore plausible, Topics. The former is the lot of very few. The latter is common; and fit enough for common affairs—to buy and sell, to teach Grammar and the like; but is utterly unfit to meddle with Politics, Divinity and Philosophy. But Enthusiasm is a sort of Instinct, in those who possess it, that operates, like all Instincts, better than a mean Species of Reason.

It is true indeed that enthusiasm often misleads us. So does reason too. Such is the Condition of our Nature; and we can't help it. But I believe that we act most when we act with all the Powers of our Soul; when we use our Enthusiasm to elevate

---

[1] I.e. that religion is to help us in worldly things.

and expand our Reasoning; and our Reasoning to check the Roving of our Enthusiasm.

As God has made all his Creatures active, He has made Man principally so. Many of our actions that compose our principal Duties are difficult, attended with trouble, and often with Danger. But action is influenced by Opinion—and our Notion of things; and nothing but strong and confirmed Opinion can lead to resolute Action. Therefore doubt and Scepticism were no more made for Man than Pride and Positiveness; for no Action, or but feeble and imperfect essays towards action, can arise from dubious Notions and fluctuating Principles.

[In the MS. the next piece follows on, after a ruled line, on the same page.]

## [ 17 ]

This piece is almost certainly by Edmund Burke (see Introduction, p. 8).

ও·

## *RELIGION*

### [By Edmund Burke]

If there be a God such as we conceive, He must be our Maker.

If he is our Maker, there is a Relation between us.

If there be a Relation between us, some Duty must arise from that Relation, since [we] cannot conceive that a reasonable Creature can be placed in any Relation that does not give rise to some Duty.

This Relation betwixt God and Man, is that Man has received several Benefits but can return none. That he may suffer all Manner of Mischief, but can return none, or by himself avert none.

Therefore by no *act* can he perform this Duty; but he can by the Sentiments of his Mind.

Where we have received good, 'tis natural to Praise.

Where we hope good, it is natural to pray.

Where we fear Evil, 'tis natural to deprecate it.

*This is the foundation of Religion.*

We have a Relation to other Men.

We want many things compassable only by the help of other beings like ourselves.

They want things compassable within our Help.

We love these beings and have a Sympathy with them.

If we require help, 'tis reasonable we should give help.

If we love, 'tis natural to do good to those whom we love.

Hence one Branch of our Duties to our fellow Creatures is active—Hence Benevolence.

*This is the foundation of Morality.*

Morality does not necessarily include Religion, since it concerns only our Relation with Men.

But Religion necessarily includes Morality, because the Relation of God as a Creator is the same to other Men as to us.

If God has placed us in a Relation attended with Duties, it must be agreeable to him that we perform those Duties.

*Hence Moral Duties are included in Religion, and enforced by it.*

If God has provided fatally for all things, we may honour him but we can neither love him, fear him, nor hope in Him. For there is no object for those Passions.

This would reduce all worship to praise only, and Gratitude.

Gratitude is an inert Principal, because it concerns only things done.

Hope and fear are the Springs of everything in us, because they look to the future about which, only, Mankind can be sollicitous. To take away Providence would therefore be to take away Religion.

The Arguments against Providence are from our *Reasonings*, observing a certain order in the works of God. There is nothing at all in our natural feelings against it.

There is a great deal in our natural feelings for it.

All Dependant Beings that have a Sense of their Dependence naturally cry out to their Superiour for assistance.

No man can act uniformly as if a fatality governed everything.

Men do not naturally conceive that, when they are strongly actuated to call upon a Superior, that [*sic*] they cannot be heard; they do not conceive that they have Passions which have no Purpose.

They naturally measure their Duties to the Divinity by their own wants and their feelings, and not by abstract Speculations.

In the one they cannot be deceived, in the other they may.

One is taken from the Nature of God which we do not understand, the other from our own which we understand better.

Metaphysical or Physical Speculations neither are, or ought to be, the Grounds of our Duties; because we can arrive at no certainty in them. They have a weight when they concur with our own natural feelings; very little when against them.

The Ends of a transitory Animal may be answered without any knowledge of a God. They are so answered in Beasts.

Men have some knowledge of God.

*Hence we presume other Ends are to be answered.*

Man has Ideas of Immortality, and wishes for it; he does not think he has Ideas and Wishes, for no End.

*Hence he presumes he may be Immortal.*

Man is sensible he has Duties; that the Performance of these Duties must be agreeable to God; That being agreeable to God is the way to be happy.

Experience shows him that the Performance of these Duties does not give him happiness in Life;—therefore He concludes that they must make him happy after Death; and that for that Reason, something in him must survive.

He sees that this Notion is favourable to the performance of all his Duties, and that the Contrary notion is unfavourable to it.

He observes that this Notion tends to perfect his Nature; that the contrary tends to sink him to a level of Inferiour Natures.

In disputed Questions those Notions that tend to make him better and happier, to bind him to his fellow Creatures, and to his Creator and to make him a more excellent Creature, are true rather than the Contrary. These Arguments are taken from within; the others are foreign.

If his Soul survives after Death; it does not appear why it should not live for ever.

If the Soul lives for ever, the Space of time spent in this Life is inconsiderable. It is therefore reasonable that it should take up but the smallest part of our Attention.

We do not know how far our relation to other Men shall continue after Death.

We know that our Relation to God must continue the same after Death.

We know therefore that our Duty to God is of more Moment than our Attention to ourselves or others.

It is natural to suppose that what goes first in the order of Nature should produce what follows it.

It is therefore reasonable to conclude that our Performance of our Duty here must make our fate afterwards.

It is reasonable that the smallest part of anything should be destined for the Uses of the whole, rather than that the whole should be employed for the purpose of a part.

It is therefore reasonable to suppose that our Actions here are made the *Causes* of our future happiness or Misery, and not that our future Misery and Happiness are designed as the Sanctions of our Duties here.

*Hence it is that this Life is a Preparation for the next.*

Hence it is that we ought not to emmerse ourselves too much in the things which make us consider this Life as our all.

Hence it is that for this Purpose we ought to deny ourselves; since an Indulgence in Pleasures here removes our Attention from further Objects, and weakens our Desire for them.

We may have observed that the Passions which arise from self love frequently clash with those Duties which arise from our Relation to other Men.

But less mischief arises from a restraint on our desires, than from indulging them to the prejudice of others.

Thus self-Denial becomes the second of the Pillars of Morality.

This is the more austere part of our Duty, and the most difficult.

If we depend upon a Superior being, it is but just that we should pray to him; because we have no other means of sufficiently expressing our Dependence; though he should already be sufficiently apprised of our wants, and willing to supply them.

If we depend upon any Superior being, it is reasonable that we should trust in him, though we do not see the Motives and tendencies of his Actions. Good Will even among Men could not be supported otherwise.

If we have Reason to suppose that he has proposed any thing, we ought to believe it firmly, though we should not thoroughly comprehend the Nature of the things proposed; otherwise we break off our Dependence as much as we should our Connexion with Men if we refused them all Credit.

God has given us a knowledge of himself, and we believe that knowledge to be of some Importance to us.

We therefore ought not to imagine it impossible that he may be willing to give us some further knowledge of his Nature or his Will.

Neither is it reasonable that we should judge it impossible for him to find fit Means of communicating this knowledge.

If he intends to communicate such knowledge, the best Proofs of such a Design are such acts of Power as can leave us no Doubt of their coming from God; for thus it is we know that he exist[s] and that he is all powerful and all-wise.

God has for the most Parts made Men the Instruments of all the Good he does to Men.

Most of their strength is from mutual Assistance.

Most of their knowledge from mutual Instruction.

There is a principal of Credit, or faith, in Man to Man without which this Assistance and Instruction would be impracticable.

Therefore Human Testimony is the strongest Proof we can have of anything; and leaves no doubt when it is very strong.

That there is such a City as Rome, is a Proposition of which we can doubt less than that the Square of the Hypotenuse is equal to the Squares of the two Sides, even when the latter is demonstrated.

The highest Degree of testimony leaves less doubt than Demonstration.

Besides the force of it is more easily and generally comprehended.

If God has revealed anything by evident Proofs from his Power, and that these Proofs of Power are conveyed to us by as high a Degree of Testimony as the thing can bear, we ought to believe it.

If the thing[s] conveyed be intended to last in the world, there must be means taken to make them last; there must be Men appointed to teach them,—and Books written to record.

There should be some evident marks of the Designation of

such Men; that all may know, who they are that teach this Doctrine.

These Men should be compellable to teach it; lest the knowledge of these truths might depend upon Caprice. There must therefore be a Society for this Purpose.

[ 18 ]

This dialogue appears to be in the hand of William Burke throughout. Its form of humour, also, is perhaps more typical of William than of Edmund. Its authorship must remain doubtful.

∾

## A DIALOGUE

An.[acreon?] How now, Gentlemen, what means this knot of you? You will lose your Character as Lovers and Poets to be thus together. You should be single in the Groves; lamenting your Mistresses or courting your muses.

Ov.[id] Why, faith Anachreon, I own it is not consistent with our former Lives; but to tell you the truth we intend fairly to quit the trade of loving. We would fain leave off our follies; for sure it is time for those who are now two thousand Years dead to be a little wiser.

Tibul.[lus] Nay; in that we do no more than all old fellows who leave their follies when they can practice them no longer. For my part (and I fear you found it out sooner than I did) I am quite exhausted. All my Sighs, Ardours, dying darts, brilliant Eyes, rosy Cheeks, marble bosoms, despair, Agonies, Deaths, Hells I have said so often over that I am e'en tired of them; and am resolved to turn sober, since I can no longer play the fool with Success.

An. To play the fool with Success you ought to do as I did,

not with a serious face, but as in drollery. It is like a mounte-bank and his Merry Andrew. One acts sillily in a grave way, and the other in a brisk. Now they are both blockheads; the Master only passes for a fool, the servant for a Wit.

Ov. So thou wert never seriously in Love?

An. No not I. Pray were you? Now speak honestly; consider you are dead.

Ov. Is Julia within Ear shot?

Tib. No, no, all the women are gone to view the New Irish-man I think they call him, one Maclane; a fellow that made his way to this world through the Gallows, and lived by his Gallantrys in the other.

An. Irishman prythe[e], what is that?

Tib. Why, they are the most successful lovers now in the upper Regions; and have the Art of making deeper Impressions on their Mistresses than ever we could boast by our Songs and Odes. This fellow was the most famous among them; it is whispered that the women above were so solicitous to save him, that their Husbands resolved to hang him; and that Curiosity which sticks to women above and below, has carried all our Women to learn of this fellow this new method of getting at a woman's heart; so that our love songs and all that, will soon be disregarded. The novelty, at least, of the thing will detain them long enough to give you time enough, Ovid, to answer Anacreon's question. Answer it fairly.

Ov. Why there is a distinction to be made; for a man may be [in?] Love as a — that is, as a man may say;

Anac. Oh, no bogling about it;—truth, it seems, sticks as much in your throat as the Grape stone did in mine. Out with it.

Ov. Then to speak plain, I never was in Love.

Tib. Nor I!

An. and G.[allus] Nor I!

An. So, so! And what the Devil tempted you to pour such

a heap of nonsense on the world, that has made so many Men mad, and so many women whores?

Ov. To get the reputation of a Wit, and the enjoyment of a Princess.

Tib. That I might be thought soft and delicate.

G. And I, that I might extort a pretty panegyrick from Virgil.

An. Choice motives surely; but pray, Mr Tibullus, may I be so bold to ask the real name of the lady you pretended to be in Love with.

Tib. Really it is so long ago that I have forgot it.

Ov. And who was your Lycorea my Lord Gallus?

Gal. Now, as I hope to drink of Lethe, you either are grown very dull since you left the world, or affect to be so. Don't you know, that true Wits, such as we are, have no Mistress but fame? That some court her with heroicks, some with tragicks, some with Satyres, and such as we with amorous Madrigals and Elegies? We set up for this Dulcinea of our Imaginations some such Creature as neither ever was or ever could be; a Lady made up of Rubies, Pearls, Roses, lillies and what not. Her we be-rhime from head to foot, not leaving even her little toe-nail without an Epigram. When we have done with herself we then proceed to her household furniture; make sonnets on her fan, Gloves, looking-Glass and Cabinet. Then we celebrate the happiness of her bird, Lap dog, and Monkey; or if we happen to be a little in the Spleen, we make woeful Elegies on the deaths of the said Animals; we ask them why they should leave so sweet a mansion as her Chamber; and conclude at last that the greatest joys are but of short duration; and all this so pathetically, that it is impossible to read them without tears; when at the same time there never was such a Lady, Parrot, Lap-Dog or Monkey in the world.

Ov. Truely Gallus says right, and I think the matter appears to me so ridiculous, that I am resolved entirely to leave it off, or learn from somebody how to practice it better. I hope, however, that our weakness in this point has had no Imitators.

*An.* No Imitators! What do you think of the world? Do You think Nature knows how to lose a kind? They live on our fragments; and, like poor Servants, pride themselves in the Cloaths we are ashamed to wear.

*Tib.* But can it be possible that the world in all this time has not grown wiser, or at least improved in the folly?

*An.* Very possible! You shall see a packet my friend Mercury brought me the other day;—but I am wrong, you shall not see it—it may provoke you too much; for it seems they are our Children, but O Pluto! how degenerate!

*Ov.* Let's see them, however,—or at least the most tolerable of them; for I burn with Curiosity.

*An.* Well, we'll lay aside this huge packet entitled Sonnetti. These Madrigals, too, we shall not open; this enormous bundle of Songs would set us distracted. But here are others a little more tolerable, written by some Authors lately come among us. If [they] produce no better Credentials than those, they shall never be admitted into the Lovers' quarter, however they may be received by the wits. As for those parcels we have put by, we shall consign them to Rhadamanthus, to be read to the damned Criticks and Poets under his Jurisdiction. You, Tibullus, who have [a] soft Voice, begin and read—

*Tib.* 'Ye cooling Shadows'—

*An.* Oh fye! fye! this rude masculine Voice won't do at all. One would think you were going to thunder out Arma Virumq[ue]. A little more on the languishing;—'Ye Cooling Shadows'—so; incline the head on the left shoulder a little—so —so pretty well—

*Tib.* Ye cooling Shadows and refreshing Streams,
    Defence from Phoebus, not from Cupid's, Beams.

*Ov.* Very very pretty.

Gal. Oh you must allow such a speech to Courtiers; who are always fonder of showing their Wit than proving their passion.

An. Courtiers—Why it is a Shepherd who speaks.

Gal. Oh, I beg his Shepherdship's pardon; but he is e'en to well bred for his office; he is like a masquerade Strephon that knows not how to act his part—

Ov. Enough, Enough, Tibellus! We have heard sufficient to make us ashamed of what we have done; it is like the Sins of our Youth that come to torment us with the memory of them in our Old Days. But, if I mistake not, I see Sapho coming hither thro the Trees; she seldom favours us with her Company; tho' no one can so well inform us on the subject we are now on, as She who died for love. Go, Tibellus, and speak to her.

Tib. Alas I am quite ashamed; she has a great dislike to me. But let Ovid; he has the Art of Love upon his tongue, the genteelest address, and the happiest Impudence.

Ov. Well, for your Panegyrick I will go—and She is no woman[1] if I don't bring her.—But she is just with us.— Madam, I am deputed by these Gentlemen to speak. They have, indeed, hitherto been allowed Masters in the Art of Love, and it is from Sapho's experienced judgement only that they could hope for Instruction.

Sap. Waste not my time, talker; nor stop my Steps, unless you can tell me of Phaon. I seek the ingrate who stole from me while I slept yonder among the Lillies. But since Your topick is love, and as Anachreon is on Company, I will spare you a few moments. What would You?

An. Madam, we desire instruction in the Art of writing love Verses.

Sap. You show by your desire that Instructions can do you no good. The first precept is—'to be in Love' and all the rest is

[1] Women in MS.

easy. Don't we every [day] see Men who are no Poets, Yet inspired by this passion, do wonders, while you, whose title to Wit no one disputes, are foiled by your Inferiours when you would write on this subject? In matters of this nature you should invoke Cupid; not the Muses. For here well turned Compliments are nothing. For in true love, as in true friendship, they are not used. Nor are deep researches into the Cause of your passion, nor fine reflections on it a bit better. That wound is not felt when you can dress it yourself; nor will being witty on your misery serve you. For be assured, that till you have lost all your wit, You are not in love. Why is love always painted a Child, but that he reduces all to the simplicity of Children? Why is he painted blind? If you be at leisure to indulge Description, also if you once find yourself in the describing humour, throw down your Pen. You write without the Muse's leave. A Sigh, A tear, Silence itself, shows more love than all your Eloquence. In short, I know no precept to give You, but to be in love really; and then, as you have some talents, write ill if you can. But, fool that I am, why do I waste my time with these talkers? Perhaps some happier, more watchful, maid engages my Phaon. Away, away!

An. What's the matter, Gentles?

Ov. I wish the Irish may engage Julia. I know nothing of the Art of Love.

Tib. What will become of my Elegies?

An. Oh my friends, don't be dispirited. It is true, indeed; what she says seems to be pretty right. But then comfort yourselves, there are but few of her writings left to show the Difference. And even tho' they had all been extant, you need not have despaired of finding enough who would prefer yours to hers.

Ov. I care not,—I am resolved to write such things no more. Nothing but the heat of Youth or Violence of Passion can excuse such writing. And when they do not carry that passport along with them they are insufferable. For sure, to see an Old grave Man sit down leisurely in his Study indicting amorous Stanzas on his finger's Ends—it is so ridiculous, that I know not what name to give his venerable Dotage,—So farewel, my friends, and each grow wise at Leisure.

[ 19 ]

This piece, clearly by Edmund Burke, and inscribed as being so, is one of the most typical of his style and thought in the note-book; for example, the passage 'I have too much reverence for our nature to wish myself divested of even the weak parts of it', and many other passages. The only portion which seems to sink below his high standard is that dealing with scientific experiment,—beginning 'Perhaps the bottom of most things is unintelligible....' The rest is emphatically Edmund Burke at his best.

◦

## SEVERAL SCATTERED HINTS CONCERNING PHILOSOPHY AND LEARNING COLLECTED HERE FROM MY PAPERS. [*E.B.*][1]

[By Edmund Burke]

In our Interests we consider *ourselves* more than we ought; in our Improvements we consider ourselves too little; our learning is calculated for show not for use, and it fares accordingly; for it seldom goes further than the tongue. When we study for ourselves we have usually the advantage of show and substance too; or if we should miss the former, we shall be taught not much to regret the loss. To learn for show is like

---

[1] In pencil.

painting for complexion, it looks tawdry, lasts not long, and is no better than a Cheat.

The appearance from real learning is like a complexion had from sound health; it looks lively and natural, and is only the sign of something better.

It signifies much less what we read than how we read, and with a view to what end. To study only for its own sake is a fruitless labour; to learn only to be learned is moving in a strange Circle. The End of learning is not knowledge but virtue; as the End of all speculation should be practice of one sort or another. It is owing to inattention to this that we so often see men of great Erudition immersed as deeply as any in the passions, prejudices, and vain opinions of the vulgar; nay we often see them more servile, more proud, more opinionative, fonder of money, more governed by vanity, more afraid of Death, and captivated more by little appearances and trifling distinctions. In these two last particulars I have often observed it, and always with wonder.

It is worth observing that when anything not a principal itself, and cultivated only as an accessory to something else, is diverted from its proper end, it not only does not promote that end, but it goes a great way to destroy it.[1] The Gymnastic exercises among the Greeks were undoubtedly designed to form their people to war; and they seem well calculated for that purpose. But when they forgot that purpose, when they made that art acquiesce in itself, when they sought a reputation from the exercise alone, it lost its use; and the professed Wrestlers always made the worst Soldiers.[2] Those who make a trade of Tumbling are never very remarkable for their agility in any other way; and in the little Course of my own experience, I have always observed of your prodigious and ostentatious memories that they served for little else than prodigy and

[1] Cf. no. 16, 'Religion...as a State Engine'.
[2] Cf. Scott in 'Count Robert of Paris'.

ostentation. It has happened in a manner not unlike this to learning. Knowledge is the Culture[1] of the mind; and he who rested there, would be just as wise as he who should plough his field without any intention of sowing or reaping.

There are two sorts of men who hold learning in but a moderate esteem. The first are they who having gone through a long Course of Study and having mastered the principles of most Sciences, find how weak and fallacious the Grounds of many are, and how uncertain the very best. They follow a noble Chase with much delight and no small pains, and at last find the pursuit was better than the Game. The second sort are they who know nothing at all of Literature, and despise all the advantages of Study in comparison of their own natural Genius. These two sorts of men concur in much the same opinions, but on quite different reasons; and therefore with quite different Esteem. For the opinion of one arises from depth of thought and humility; the other from profound ignorance and the most intollerable pride. To slight an advantage a man eminently possesses, is no common strain of modesty: to despise what we don't know is folly and impudence. A man ought, like Solomon, to know all things from the Cedar to the Hyssop before he presumes to declare that all Knowledge is Vanity.

Those who make general objections against learning; those who rail at any particular Art, as that of Lawyers or Physicians, in the gross, those who contend that Beasts are wiser than men, are none of them very sollicitous to prove their points in good earnest; they only want to show their parts, and are best mortified by not contesting with them.

As learning in some measure answers to the experience of Old age, it seems to produce something of its querulous disposition too. I do not know any discourse worse received than com-

[1] Culture in the original sense of ploughing for sowing later.

plaints of the times; and I think with some reason; as they usually begin with our own misfortunes and end with them. But such complaints least of all become men of Learning, who by some fatality are always stunning us with the reproaches of the age they live in, and the little encouragement they receive. And it will ever be so whilst men propose to themselves any other views in Learning than the regulation of their minds and their own inward content and repose. If we consider the matter rightly, what reward should I expect for doing myself the greatest service imaginable? If I complain of want of encouragement in this way, it is a sure sign I deserve none. If my Studies are not of such a nature as to enable me to make a figure in the world, or to acquire some better possession instead of it, what have I been doing? And in what a light do I present myself?

We ought rather to be learned *about* Sciences than *in* them (I don't speak here of the particular profession of any). That is, we ought, if possible, rather to master those principles that govern almost all of them than to sift into those particulars that direct and distinguish each of them separately. By these means we can extend our views much more considerably; we keep our minds open, and prevent that littleness and narrowness that almost inevitably attends a confined commerce with any Art or Science however noble in itself. I remember a preface to some book of Heraldry wherein the Author, after giving due commendation to his own Studies, passes a severe Censure on those who are weak enough to mis-spend their time in such trivial pursuits as those of philosophy and poetry, neglecting an art of so much delight in the Study, and advantage in the application, as Heraldry.

Confined reading and company are the Greatest Sources of pride that I know; and I am sure any knowledge that carries this taint along with it does not make amends for the mischief it brings. If a man be a poor narrow minded Creature what does it avail whether he is a Logician or a Shoemaker, a Geometrician or a Taylor? If he has the narrow views of a Mechanic, he is as far from being a philosopher as the mechanic, and farther too, if the other chances to have from nature a more generous way of thinking.

There is inseparably annexed to any confined Studies a number of false admirations that a more general knowledge would go a great way to Cure. When a man is conversant in all the variety of Arts and Sciences, in the Stories, opinions, Customs, manners, atchievements of all ages and all nations, it must by a sure consequence wear away those little prejudices of little parties that Cause such heats and animosities amongst mankind; it must lessen something of that extravagant admiration of power and riches that intoxicates us to our ruin, and overturns the peace and innocence of our lives. It might perhaps humble us, and abate something of our confidence in our opinions, if, after taking a view of the rise and fall of kingdoms, we observed those of science; to see it rise from chance, grow by industry, strengthen by contention, refine by subtilty and ease, fall then into nicety, Error, Guess,—and, dissolving at last, make way for new Systems, which rise by the same means, and fall by the same fortune. Whatever tends to humble us, tends to make us wiser. Whatever makes us wiser, makes us better, and easier, and happier.

I would make an ingenuous and liberal turn of mind the End of all learning and wherever I don't see it I should doubt the reality of the knowledge. For the End of all knowledge ought to be the bettering us in some manner; and whoever has a sour, splenetick, unsocial, malevolent Temper; who is haughty in his own acquirements and contemptuous of others; ostentatious of his knowledge, positive in his Tenets, and abusive to those who differ from him; he may be a Scholar,—and indeed most of those called Scholars are something in this Character,

—but sure he is not a man of learning, nor a philosopher. The more he vaunts his reading, the more loudly he proclaims his ignorance. If a deep and general knowledge does not make a man diffident and humble, no human means, I believe, can do it.

To attempt a general knowledge ought not to be thought too bold an undertaking; to have many things in hand will rather advance us in Each, whilst they relieve one another; and prevent that satiety which arises from a confined application, and which can have no relief but in Idleness or some other Study, And which is to be preferred, everyone may judge.

There is certainly, besides, some connexion in all the Sciences which makes them mutually advance one another; though I allow not so much as some contend for. But one of the Strongest reasons I have for admitting great variety into our Studies, and a passing in a pretty Quick Succession from one to another, is that it helps to form that *versatile ingenium* which is of very great use in Life,—Not to be so possessed with any subject, but that we should be able at pleasure to quit it, to turn to another, so to a third, to resume the first again, and to follow the occasion with a suppleness that may suit the infinite intricacy that occurs in many sorts of Business and employments. For we ought if possible to keep all our talents subservient to the uses of Life, and not to make ourselves the Slaves of any of them. Those who lay out their whole time on any one Science, are apt to be carried away by it; and are no longer their own masters so far as to decide when and where, and in what measure they shall indulge their Speculations; and therefore are not so generally fit for the world.

There is great reason to believe that being engaged in business is rather of service to Speculative knowledge than otherwise; because perhaps the mind can do more in sudden starts than in an even progression. Experience may show that an entire application to study alone is apt to carry men into unprofitable Subtilities and whimsical notions. Man is made for Speculation and action; and when he pursues his nature he succeeds best in both.

I am not moved with what it is common for people to advance about superficial learning. A man who does not seek a reputation from his knowledge, will be indifferent whether it be thought deep or shallow provided it be of any real use to him. One may know all the maxims of a Science, be perfectly conversant in their Grounds, ready in the reasonings about them, and know all that has been thought, written, or experimented on that Subject, and yet have but a superficial knowledge in that Science. Another who knows but few of its principles, if yet he can extend them, can multiply their resources, can strike out something new, can remedy some defect, he has a deeper knowledge in the Science than the other, if this other should not be able to advance its landmarks,—as thousands well conversant in Arts cannot do, and who therefore have a more superficial knowledge, because a less useful one. And such is the weakness of the human mind, that it is found, a great acquaintance and readiness in what is already known in any branch of Learning is rather of prejudice than use in extending it.

It is common with men of a small understanding to think nothing of any use, that is not particularly and avowedly designed for use, and apparently so. But in fact there are things that aim obliquely at their end that often hit it more surely. I speak this of such who depreciate the ornamental parts of Learning as Eloquence, Poetry, and such like—and consider them merely as matter of ornament. I look on them in quite a different light, because I always consider the Chief use of Learning is to implant an elegant disposition into the mind and manners and to root out of them everything sordid, base or illiberal. I conceive that the polite arts are rather better calculated for this purpose than any others; and this for the very reason that some condemn them; because they apply to the passions, in which, more than in any faults of reasoning, the Sources of all our Errors lie.

Those who speak in favour of these studies, on the other hand, do not seem to me truly to discern wherein their advantage consists. Say they, moral precepts when graced with the advantages of Eloquence, invite the inattentive, and by being mixed with something pleasureable, make a deeper impression. It is true they do so; but in fact the great powers of Eloquence and poetry, and the great Benefits that result from them, are not in giving precepts but creating habits. For the preceptive part of poetry makes but a small part of it in all poems; and none at all in many; and yet they all have their use. For the mind when it is entertained with high fancies, elegant and polite sentiments, beautiful language, and harmonious sounds, is modelled insensibly into a disposition to elegance and humanity. For it is the bias the mind takes that gives direction to our lives; and not any rules or maxims of morals and behaviour. It imitates what is called the natural Temper best; and this is the best guide and guard we can have in every Virtue. For though rules, fear, interest, or other motives may induce us to virtue, it is the virtue of a bad soil, harsh and disagreeable.

Most Books, prove, affirm, demonstrate; they come with settled notions to us, and make us settle ours too early. We are too apt to take our parties in everything when our Judgement is very unripe and make the reasoning of our mature years subservient to the rashness of our Youth. I am almost tempted to think we ought to learn not so much to cure our Doubts, of which we have too few, as to learn how to doubt.

We daily hear the words, 'tis impossible, 'tis absurd, 'tis unreasonable, 'tis contradiction, used on many occasions with equal hardiness and ignorance; and that on every side of Questions extremely dark and puzzling, and which seem as it were calculated to suspend and confound the human understanding. If a man seriously set about regarding his opinions of things in several periods of his life, he would see what he thought in one part of it impossible was easy; what he thought absurd, he now finds highly reasonable; how his experience reverses his notions; makes him adopt what he rejected and reject what he was fondest of. These considerations one would think might tend to humble the understanding and make it Cautious and diffident.—Such a review is sometimes made; but with a very different Effect; we view the littleness of our former notions with an exultation on our present Growth; we Triumph in the comparison; and never recollect that we are to tread the same Circle again; affording matter of contempt in our present Triumph to our later, God knows whether wiser, Schemes of things. We should take a quite contrary Course—I once was sure; I now find I was mistaken; I am going to be very positive again; can I say a few years more may not show me that I was positive in an Error?

To have the mind a long time lost in Doubts and uncertainties may have the same Effect on our understandings that fermentation has on liquors. It disturbs them for a while, but it makes them both the Sounder and clearer ever after.

We read too much; and our studies being remote from the occasions of Life cannot so easily be mixt with them afterwards. It were to be wished that matters of moment made a larger part in the conversations even of the greatest men. It is but reasonable that our general conduct should be a good deal modelled by the general Sense of the publick; and that unfortunately leads to amusements, trivial or worse; but I would willingly give something to reason as well as Custom; I would be its humble Servant but not its Slave. What we learn in Conversation is in some way of a better kind than that we draw from

Books; and it certainly goes further towards influencing our Conduct. Discourse is nearer to action and mixes more with it than mere reading, and surely Philosophy of every sort is naturally pleasing to the mind; it is not excluded from conversation because it is sour and pedantick, but it is apt to be sour and pedantick, when it is excluded from conversation.

The more a man's mind is elevated above the vulgar the nearer he comes to them in the simplicity of his appearance, speech, and even not a few of his Notions. He knows his reason very well and therefore he is suspicious of it. He trusts his passions more on some occasions; he reins them, but does not fetter them. A man who considers his nature rightly will be diffident of any reasonings that carry him out of the ordinary roads of Life; Custom is to be regarded with great deference especially if it be an universal Custom; even popular notions are not always to be laughed at. There is some general principle operating to produce Customs, that is a more sure guide than our Theories. They are followed indeed often on odd motives, but that does not make them less reasonable or useful. A man is never in greater danger of being wholly wrong than when he advances far in the road of refinement; nor have I ever that diffidence and suspicion of my reasonings as when they seem to be most curious, exact, and conclusive. Great subtelties and refinements of reasoning are like spirits which disorder the brain and are much less useful than ordinary liquors of a grosser nature; I never would have our reasoning too much dephlegmatic, much less would I have its pernicious activity exerted on the forms and ceremonies that are used in some of the material Businesses and more remarkable changes of Life. I find them in all nations, and at all times; and therefore I judge them suitable to our nature, and do not like to hear them called fopperies. Our fathers, ruder indeed than we, and, if not instructed, at least not misled, practised them; we should follow them. But they ought not to affect us beyond their just value. When Diogenes was dying, his friends desired to know how he would have his Body disposed of. 'Throw it into the fields,' says he. They objected that it might be liable to be devoured by wild Beasts. 'Then set my Staff by me to drive them off.' One answered, 'You will be then insensible and unable to do it.' 'So shall I be' (sayd he) 'of their injuries.'

I like the vivacity of the Turn in this Story. The philosophy is shewy but has no substance; for to what would he persuade us by this odd example? Why, that our Bodies being after Death neither capable of pain nor pleasure, we should not trouble our heads about them. But let this pass into a general principle, and thence into a general practice, and the ill consequence is obvious. The wisdom of nature, or rather providence, is very worthy of admiration in this, as in a thousand other things, by working its ends by means that seem directed to other purposes. A man is anxious and sollicitous about the fate of his body which he knows can have no feeling. He never considers what a nuisance it would be to Society if it was exposed. He considers such an event as personally terrible; and he does piously for others what he would wish done for himself.

It is not easily conceived what use funeral ceremonies (for my story led me to think) are to mankind. Triffling as they may seem, they nourish humanity, they soften in some measure the rigour of Death, and they inspire humble, sober and becoming thoughts. They throw a decent Veil over the weak and dishonourable circumstances of our Nature. What shall we say to that philosophy, that would strip it naked? Of such sort is the wisdom of those who talk of the Love, the sentiment, and the thousand little dalliances that pass between the Sexes, in the gross way of mere procreation. They value themselves as having made a mighty discovery; and turn all pretences to delicacy into ridicule. I have read some authors who talk of the

Generation of mankind as getting rid of an excrement; who lament bitterly their being subject to such a weakness. They think they are extremely witty in saying it is a dishonourable action and we are obliged to hide it in the obscurity of night. It is hid it's true, not because it is dishonourable but because it is mysterious. There is no part of our condition, but we ought to submit to with Cheerfulness. Why should I desire to be more than man? I have too much reverence for our nature to wish myself divested even of the weak parts of it. I would not wish, as I have heard some do, that I could live without eating or sleeping. I rather thank providence that has so happily united the subsistence of my body with its satisfaction. When we go into another State we shall have means fitted to it, with equal wisdom no doubt. At the present we ought to make the best of our Condition; and improve our very necessities, our wants, and imperfections, into Elegancies;—if possible, into virtues.

The common people are puzzled about extraordinary Phenomena, and wonder at nothing else. The learned wonder not at uncommon things; 'tis about the most ordinary things they are puzzled and perplexed. They can account for earthquakes and eclipses, but doubt of their seeing feeling hearing etc. In reasoning about abstruse matters and the assent we give to Propositions concerning them, we don't sufficiently distinguish between a Contrariety and a Contradiction. No man in his Senses can agree to a Contradiction; but an apparent, nay a real, Contrariety in things, may not only be proposed and believed, but proved beyond any reasonable doubt. Most of our Enquiries, when carried beyond the very Superficies of things, lead us into the greatest Difficulties and we find qualities repugnant to each other whenever we attempt to dive into the Manner of Existence.

Nec tamen istas questiones Physicorum contemnandas puto.

Est enim Animarum Ingeniorumque naturale quoddam quasi pabulum, consideratio contemplatioque Naturae.[1]

Perhaps the bottom of most things is unintelligible; and our surest reasoning, when we come to a certain point, is involved not only in obscurity but contradiction. Suppose we divide a Body into many parts; yet each part will have *Length, Breadth, Thickness*; and so will every part of those Parts, and so ad infinitum. But those Qualities are sensible properties, and when they do not affect the Sense, we cannot be certain that these Qualities exist; since they do not operate; for we know of their Existence but by their Operation. If it be said that they grow too small for the sense, I believe these words are not well understood; for small and great are only in reference to the Impression made on the Sensory; and if there is no Impression I don't see how any-thing can be called *great* or *Small*. So that if they exist, they must have other Properties, Since those they have are not sensible Qualities. Again all Bodies being composed originally of Minute parts, they may in that Separate State have qualities different from what they have in the aggregate: and may be otherwise coloured, figured etc.

It is a fact well known to those who are conversant in Metallurgy that Copper and Lapis Calaminaris when mixed weighs more in the compound called Brass than they did before; that is, that a pound of Copper and a pound of Lapis Cal. make more than two pounds of Brass. A very astonishing fact; and which seems to shake the Credit of that established maxim in Physick, that the weight of Bodies is as the Quantity of Matter. Here in

---

[1] This quotation appears again in the Preface (p. ix) to the 2nd edition of Burke's work on *The Sublime and Beautiful* (1759) where he writes: 'By looking into physical courses our minds are opened and enlarged; and in this pursuit, whether we take or whether we lose our game, the chase is certainly of service. Cicero...confesses its great importance to the human understanding: Est animarum ingeniorumque naturale quoddam quasi pabulum, consideratio contemplatioque Naturae.'

the fusion of these mineral Substances is an accession of weight without any increase of Matter. Nay, what is more probable, with a considerable Diminution; for in the melting of Metals, as in all Bodies exposed to fire, no mean part flies off in fume; in many cases to the great Detriment of the workers—May it not be that a Different co-aptation of Parts, and a different Operation of them one on another, and perhaps by that means on other Bodies, may increase their gravity, as by such a Diversity of Positions or Motions they acquire other Qualities which they had not before, or have them encreased or changed according to the nature of the Cause? For possibly gravity may be encreased or diminished by other means than by the encrease or Diminution of Matter. A Body of the same particles a Mile from the Surface of the Earth has not the same weight with one of equal particles a Mile within the Surface. The true Cause of this is not known, and perhaps cannot be known. The effect is called Gravity; and I would know why some as unknown unknowable Cause may not, on the Surface of the Earth, produce the same Diversity of weights in equal quantities of Matter that another Cause does in different distances. For I suppose it will not be asserted that any nearness or Distance to or from any imaginary or mathematical Point can, merely as such, have any Influence on the Qualities of Bodies: but only that some unknown Cause observes these Laws in acting. And I cannot see why another Cause, or the same Cause otherwise exerted, may not produce the same Changes in weights of Bodies by some other means, that we see evidently done by the Distance or propinquity to a certain point.

To explain myself more fully—I don't see why the fusing together of Copper and Lap. Cal. may not communicate the same Quality (with regard to Gravity) to the Mixture, Brass, that they would have separately, if raised to 50 yards from the Ground, and compared with the same Quantity of the same Matter a Yard within the Surface. And surely effects as extraordinary as the variation of Gravity in the same particles are commonly produced.

The usual way of making a Body take fire, is by applying fire to it. If no other way of firing was known we could never conceive how fire could be communicated by other means. But we know that friction too will do it; and here I must own I see no likeness in the Cause and effect, nor could I ever judge a priori that friction could produce fire. But this is active; and we wonder not, first because it is common; and next that any Violent exertions used to produce an End surprises [*sic*] us less than a more silent and insensible one. But suppose I pour together two cold liquors which immediately fume, boil and blaze. This is, I am sure, an effect I should never expect, and a more extraordinary Change by mere mixture, or juxta position, than any Change in weight can be;—as a production of a new Quality is a more striking effect than any excess or Diminution of an old one.

Sapere aude—it requires some boldness to make use of one's reason.

We ought to be earnest not anxious in our Business.

That seems to me the most uneasy state of Life when Men are placed where the high and the low meet—where they [are] distracted with the Ambition and vast Desires of the greatest and have scarce more than the Enjoyment of the lowest State.

The Information[s] we receive from Books about Business and Men are, I believe, to be but cautiously trusted; because even if they should be right, yet being written at a distance of time, tho' Nature be justly described, yet a Variation in Customes, in the Characters and Manners of the Age, of which every Age has its own, makes a great variation in the Conduct to be pursued in the Management of Affairs.

A Man is not invariably and obstinately to [be] swayed by his own Opinion, but in affairs it is still worse to have no Dependence on your own Opinion. The first may [make in MS.] make you sometimes act wrong, the second will prevent your ever acting steadily. And steadiness is the Soul of all action. But there are Men so weak that they suffer themselves to be persuaded out of their own resolution by those whom they thought to have persuaded. And they are always unsuccessful; because, in imagining themselves always ready to be informed of their Errors, they can by no possibility see their great Error, which is their being easily persuaded that their own Opinions are always Erroneous.

In writing, the wisdom of Nature ought to be strictly imitated; which has made all things necessary to our preservation in the highest Degree pleasing to our Appetites. Dry precepts and reasoning do little. It is from the imagination and will that our Errors rise, and in them, as in their first beginnings, they ought to be attacked. Men are full as inclined to Vice as to Virtue. Now suppose a piece was written describing the Nature and extent of any Vice, suppose that it shewed its Limits, described its several Species, gave Directions about the encrease and furtherance of it;—suppose this done in such a manner as to avoid carefully the Affecting any of our passions, and then see how little the reader shall be incited to profit from the Lecture. I believe very little. But then, try what a Lascivious Song will do. This is directed to the imagination and in a Moment the Desires are raised. And so undoubtedly and much more will it hold in Virtue. Therefore they who would introduce new Religions must aim at the Imagination not the Understanding. Thus Mahomet's paradise is famed for the Indulgence of all the soft Eastern passions; While in our colder Climates the Methodist, by painting hell torments in all its [*sic*] terrors,—like the Rattle-Snake does the Squirrel—terrifies the poor wretch into

his Snare. But neither Mahomet nor the Methodist have anything to do with the Understanding. To instance in the
Methodist;—all their terms with a wicked wisdom, are chosen
by them too unintelligible and inexplicable, for fear the Understanding should have any play. Thus '*the new light*', '*the inward feeling*', '*born again*'. When a reason of their faith is demanded, this cant is the answer you receive. A plain man who
can make neither head nor tail of this, desires it to be explained.
They are embarrassed. By the pride natural to the Mind of
Man they chuse rather to think you reprobate, than themselves
absurd. And thus, wraped up in terms which themselves do
not understand, but by which their Imagination is engaged,
they continue their folly.

The Action of a play ought to be like a Rack to make Actors
discover the bottom of their Souls, the most hidden part of
their Characters. Else 'tis good for little.

It is not enough that the discourses of the Actors should be
such as are not unnatural. They ought to be natural for the
time, the occasion, the person who speaks, the person spoken
to. But above all they ought to be natural to the End i.e. such
as is proper to carry on the principle Action; and natural in
such an Action.

As there are different manners of expressing knowledge,
why not a different manner of gaining it too? Quacks
prescribe but one remedy for all Constitutions. We see the
Absurdity, yet expect that the school method should suit all
Geniuses. Their Masters are too much above them, their
play-fellows too much on a level. From the first they will
not learn much, from the latter they can learn nothing. They
are expected to be more at their Books than they chuse; and
less is attempted in Conversation with them than they are
capable of.

As those who draw charts mark the Sands and Rocks as well as the safe harbours, why should not Philosophers tell us the ill success, as well as the good, of their Experiments?

It is much more common with Men to contend in violent disputes about the Excellence of their Studies, their profession and their Countrys, than to exert themselves to do anything that may be for the Credit or advantage of them.

## [ 20 ]

This piece would seem to be inferior to the last. It is less profound and more worldly. Sections 9, 10, and 11, however, seem typical of Edmund Burke, particularly Section 9—on the Roman Catholic and Protestant religions. The earlier sections are almost like a reflection of other people's thought; while the end of the piece (from Section 15), seems to 'tail off' considerably. The writing, also, in the MS. appears to change from the beginning of Section 8, 'Frequent court martials...', onwards. The sections we have praised are, however, not in Edmund's handwriting. The piece is somewhat of a puzzle. Is it, perhaps, partly by Edmund and partly by William Burke, and copied out half by one and half by the other, without discrimination between their respective contributions?

In the original the sections are only differentiated by stars. We have replaced each star by a number for greater clearness in referring to them.

⌒

# SOME POLITICAL SCATTERED
# OBSERVATIONS

[Almost certainly in the main by Edmund Burke]

(1) Every man's Success must be owing in a great measure to the opinion men have of him.

An opinion of probity does most with the people, an opinion of Ability does best at *Court*.

(2) Eloquence has great power in popular States, reserve and prudence in Monarchies.

(3) Public affairs cannot be carried on without dissembling. In republics the *Simulatio* is most profitable.

In Courts *Dissimulatio* is more in use and of more service.[1]

(4) The greater number of Counsellors the less freedom and variety of opinions are usually found; great multitudes are incapable of acting separately; they usually move under a few leaders; and these headships are sure to give rise to envy and faction. When the number is small, each man singly considered is of more weight; is better heard; and more difficultly corrupted. The small number enhances the price; and is apt to inspire each person with a greater sense of his own dignity and importance. It is much more easy to move a crowd to some unreasonable resolution, than but three Jury-men of tolerable understanding. The first affected is usually the weakest person; and in the fluctuating of a public assembly, any man that stirs with any vigour is certainly followed,—even the knowing being hurried away by the Clamour, the warmth, and Weight of the multitude. A Crowd is like a great water which quite fills its banks; these always break at the weakest part; and though

---

[1] *Simulatio* means an assertion of something that does not exist; *dissimulatio* means a false account of something that does exist. This is described in the pentameter 'quod non est simulat, dissimulatque quod est' (one simulates what does not exist, and one dissimulates what does exist).

the breach should be but small at first, all the water running that way will make it sufficient to let in a deluge on the Country.

(5) A prince ought never to settle any difference with his Subjects in Arms by treaty, on pretence of saving Effusion of Blood. For by doing this the name of rebellion (a thing powerful against any party) is in a manner cancelled; and an aptness is ever after left in the people to rebel. Witness the ill-success of the Scots Treaty by C.1., and the long Troubles in France which had their rise from the same management. H.7. and 8th acted always in a very different manner.

(6) A very rich prince be he never so griping, or let him acquire his riches by never so bad methods, is usually safe; a prince who is poor is always dependent and almost always odious. The necessities of the State will oblige him to recruit his Coffers at any rate, and the recruit can never last long. But in the avaritious prince, the continual encrease of his Treasure strengthens him against the murmurs his manner of raising it may create. Avarice looks like wisdom; prodigality is folly. The example of Perseus K. of Mac may seem against this. But I don't here mean an avarice that degenerates into Downright madness as his did; but that of a sensible man like H.7 or Sixtus V.

(7) It is dangerous for a Prince to suffer his Capital City to be too extensive.[1]

(8) Frequent Court Martials are wrong. The Commanders ought not to see frequent Examples of them made. Severity is necessary for the Common men, but improper to commanders. The Character itself loses its Dignity by it; and the frequency of Punishments makes them more frequently deserved. The Nobility seldom punished seldom deserves it. The Principle of a General can never be a Courage created by any fear than that of Shame.

(9) The Roman Catholic Religion must be brought into a

---

[1] Cf. Tocqueville in *L'Ancien Régime* on the too predominant position of Paris.

Country by very gradual Means; there is an Order, Discipline and Policy in it that does not suit with a sudden and tumultuous proceeding. The Protestant, on the Contrary, must be introduced suddenly, because it ought to have the force of a Novelty and lay hold on the Enthusiastick part of the Mind, as it has not that advantage of a regular Polity. The former must be considerably advanced before it is seen. The forces of the latter ought to be made appear greater than they are. What Appears as Liberty, will warm; and ought to be pursued with Vehemence. What looks like Servitude and restraint is presently rejected by the Mind. The Advantages of order are not glaring, but when perceived are closely adhered to; and one new convert is a greater strength to these than 20 to the others. Of [*sic*] Papist to be a protestant, it is only necessary to throw off something; from Prt to become papist something must be assumed. Therefore they succeed well in making converts from Popery but not from Heathenism. On the Contrary the Catholicks succeed rather better in making Gentile than Protestant Proselytes.

(10) Great Subtelities and Refinements of reasoning are like Spirits drawn from Liquors; which disorder the Brain, and are much less useful than the ordinary Liquors, tho of a grosser Nature.

(11) To have the Mind a long time tossed in doubts and uncertainties may have the same Effect on our Understanding which fermentation has on Liquors, which tho it disturbs them for the present, makes them both the sounder and the clearer ever after.

(12) Men of bare Experience succeed well; but it is only in their particular walk, and where they know the temper of the Men they have to deal with. But Men of Letters have more general Ideas, understand things and Men more at large.—Bacon.—

At a long table a few about the head have the management; in other forms Counsellors who sit at the lower End have likewise something to do. B.

(13) Bacon's test of Abilities—Mitte ambos ad ignotos—is very just; for there are Men who without any Abilities have yet a Character only from having impudently challenged and claimed it; whilst Modest Merit has wanted Esteem.

(14) Those who come to beg a favour do ill to back it with any professions of Merit. It has an air of demanding it as a debt; which Men do not like to pay, so well as to give a Gratuity. Strict bare justice is not the most pleasing Virtue to either party; he that does it has no thanks, and he that receives it thinks he receives no favour.

(15) It is a great happiness of Youth that it heightens what is good and attones for what is bad. And to this it is owing that so many disappoint the Expectations they had raised, and fall into the common herd of Men; because too much Allowance was made at first and too little afterwards.

(16) I have been at several schools. Not one[1] out of fifty that I remember had any Capacity even for the small measure of learning to be picked up there; tho' many were excellent at other things. It is a wise Disposition of Providence that the Businesses of Life which require learning are very few. And they seem to counteract Nature who are for endowing numberless schools and colleges in every corner,[2] to force Men to learn what either they cannot, or [what] if they can, is like to be of no use to them.

(17) And of Numbers, too, who were what is called good school Scholars few, very few indeed, have made any figure in Life. And yet I do not remember one of whom there was no Expectation who has been considerable. I think those who did their Business well have been regular Men of Business, as they are called. Par neque supra.

[1] Supply 'person'.
[2] Cf. Richelieu, 'Ainsi qu'un corps qui aurait des yeux en toutes ses parties serait monstrueux, de même un état le serait il si tous ses sujets étaient savants... les politiques veulent, en un état bien réglé, plus de maîtres ès arts mécaniques que de maîtres ès arts libéraux pour enseigner les lettres' (*Œuvres du Cardinal de Richelieu*, R. Gaucheron, 1929, p. 183).

I remember my Lord Bath meeting a plain homely Man in a Coffee room; and in some discourse of school days the man observed 'Do you remember My Lord when I used to Make your Exercises for you?' 'I do indeed;' says Bath, 'you were always above me in the form. But I think, Bob, I have always been best heard in the house.' Yet I will answer for it Lord Bath was not reckoned a dull fellow at school.[1]

[ 21 ]

Professor Dixon Wecter, in printing this piece in *Edmund Burke and his Kinsmen* (see Introduction, p. 10) supplied it with Notes containing numerous references to the literature of the *Gentleman*, and added that it was evident that 'the Ethics of Aristotle, the ideals of chivalry, Castiglione, Elyot, Montaigne, Peacham and other influences colored Burke's thinking directly or at second-hand'. It may seem, however, that Burke could have written it without quite so many models. We think, also, that Wecter misunderstood the character of the piece when he wrote, 'One suspects that into this essay has crept something of the worldliness of the coffee-houses near Temple Bar and the ingenuity of the debating clubs in Fleet Street which, it is reported, young Burke frequented during his days as a Templar,' for surely the 'worldliness' in the piece is that of the 'fine Gentleman' and not of Burke himself, since he in no way identifies himself with the 'fine Gentleman' but only describes him. Indeed Wecter later concedes that 'perhaps such sentiments are not to be taken as mirroring the writer so clearly as they did in the case of the Noble lord' (meaning, we suppose, Chesterfield). In our opinion there is no reason to suppose that they 'mirror' the writer at all.

---

[1] William Pulteney, Earl of Bath, was, like William Burke, at school at Westminster; but they were not there at the same time, for Lord Bath went up to Christ Church in 1700 and William Burke not until 1747. The story of the former's career at school, however, may have been current among Westminster boys for some considerable time after he had left. This story may possibly imply that at any rate the end of this piece is by William Burke.

# THE CHARACTER OF A FINE
# GENTLEMAN. E.B.

[By Edmund Burke]

Some of the Learned have quarrelled with the vulgar notions
of a fine Gentleman; and because they thought this a Character
highly esteemable, were displeased to see it so often applied to
a sort of men they could by no means approve. They therefore
wholly excluded from this denomination all whose morals were
dissolute, though their manners were none so agreeable; and
they concluded that the man of compleat vertue was alone the
fine Gentleman.

We must trust the world to give names to Characters; to
change and transpose the distinctions Custom has settled,
would not be an improvement of knowledge, but an abuse of
words. Let us see then, what sort of men they are, who are
generally termed fine Gentlemen, and endeavour to settle with
ourselves a notion of this Character. But a Character is too
complete a thing to be drawn into a Definition. We may acquire a much better Idea of it from viewing it in as great a
variety of Lights as the Subject will bear.

This Character is not denominated from excellence in any
sort of Business or employment; it belongs solely to conversation, and the habitudes of pleasant Society; its Basis is politeness, whose essence is Ease: and hence it is that there is no
Character more rarely found; for easy behaviour, easy conversation, and easy writing are the hardest things in the world.
At your first Entrance into any company, the fine Gentleman is
not the person who strikes you most, and you may possibly
converse with him several times before you discover what his
excellence Is, and where It lIes.

He is no Scholar; every accomplishment he has seems to be
derived immediately from his nature; there must be no appear-

ance of any thing borrowed; to think justly, costs him no more trouble than to breathe freely. Yet he is not ignorant; he seems rather to slight books, than not to know them.

There is very little of Wit in his conversation; this is a quality that draws the admiration of company, but often at the expense of their esteem. It very soon tires; and there is such an immense distance between the heights of that, and the plainness of common discourse, that it breaks the even tenor of conversation that can alone take in the whole company and make it agreeable in all its parts.

Neither is his discourse of the humorous kind; it never raises a laugh; but yet it is not wholly averse from that Strain. There is a sort of concealed Irony that tinges his whole conversation. He entertains no extremes of opinion; he scarcely ever disputes; he is sceptical in his notions; and not fond of deep disquisitions; there is some one point in all Topics that seems to determine his judgement about them without much enquiries into other particulars. He seldom contradicts your opinions, and you will gain very little by contradicting his.

To make a man perfectly agreeable to his company he ought not to exert such Talents as may raise the envy, and consequently the uneasiness, of anybody in it. 'Tis on this principle, that the Character of a fine gentleman is not a brilliant one. There is no part of his discourse you prefer to another; and he is never the man whose bons mots are retailed in every company. His expressions are well chosen and easy, but they are not strong. There is no Glare; but there is a universal Effect produced by an infinity of fine Touches, which are imperceptible and inimitable. You may observe in lower Life, that a speaker of wise Sentences, a strenuous disputant, or one ostentatious of knowledge, never want[s] abundance of admirers; but in an higher Sphere such persons are in no great request. People of rank can brook a superiority, especially an avowed superiority, much less than others; there is a principle of politeness that forms an apparent level of their understanding. And hence I believe it is that politeness is apt sometimes to flatten into the Insipid.

The Vulgar are apt to judge of politeness by a number of ceremonious observances; but this notion is a good deal exploded amongst people of good sense and breeding. You distinguish nothing in the address of the fine Gentleman other than that it is free and unconstrained; there is a sort of openness and candour in his demeanor that invite you to that same oppenness and freedom; his Civilities and compliments are few, for there is something in professions that confound[s] a man; and a complement has not always a very pleasing Effect when it cannot be answered with Spirit.

Nothing is more disengaged than the language, the behaviour and the very looks of a perfect Gentleman; for which reason it can seldom be reached by men of Business, or professions, or those who are given to a close attention to any thing. This part grows almost spontaneously out of a plentiful fortune, the smiles of the world, and acquaintance with Courts.

Indolence is a predominant ingredient in this Character; Diligence, economy, prudence, and a consideration of the future are the virtues of men of business; and give an air of closeness and reserve, inconsistent with the perpetual Gaiety and ease that shine with such a constant Lustre in the fine Gentleman.

To be libertine in his practices and opinions is another part of his Character; but he is not a debauchee; 'tis only so much as may make him entirely a man of the world. In point of Gallantry he is no way scrupulous. The greatest liberty in his actions, and the greatest decency in his discourse are his Character in that point. Drunkenness is a Vice he abhors; but Luxury in point of eating he is not ashamed of. He may be accused of excess in Gaming; but the great Temper he preserves under his Losses, is one of his remarkable excellencies.

You see no Tincture of Vanity in his conversation; and it is a nice Eye that under that air of Affability and complaisance can discern a great deal of pride.

The fine Gentleman is never a warm friend;—it is but too true, that a Close attachment to particulars makes a man less easy and pleasing in general Society; and it is there and not in the relations of a friend, a father, a husband, or a relation, or any close connexions that a fine Gentleman shines. France is a great polisher of manners; for there they pursue publick assemblies, and neglect the satisfactions of privacy and retirement. The fine Gentleman has but little of Tenderness or what is called Good nature; a frequent feeling for others, a mixing with the unfortunate, and interesting oneself in their concerns, tends to throw a gloom on a man's Character and make it splenetick and uneven.

It is almost impossible for any man to be a fine Gentleman, who has not courage. But as such a Character is not ostentatious or affected, it is equally Essential to it to conceal this Quality. It is only to appear in a composure, formed by a confidence a man finds in himself, that he is able to prevent being disturbed in his own Course by the insolence or brutality of others. The whole Circle of Taste must be open to him; but the affected parts, the Cant of a dealer in pictures, or the Chimeras of a Virtuoso never make their appearance. Such a Character goes through Life with great Smoothness. He is praised by everybody; respected, esteemed, courted, and everything but really Loved.

I am not sure as to this last point; for he receives all the marks of Love, except the disagreeable one[s] that arise in Close intimacies, when men are undisguised and unrestrained, and give their Tempers a loose in all humours.

Perhaps this Character in all its points is not to be met. I have sometimes seen something not very far from it. To be consistent and perfect, I fancy it must be nearly as this is described. I do not mean a perfect man, for this Character has many faults; but none that do not in a good measure contribute to what we find most beautiful and pleasing in it.

## [ 22 ]

Here Burke is describing the character of one who would be thought 'a wise man' by the world in general, 'a mere wise man of this world', not one whom he himself would necessarily admire as a wise man. In this respect one may compare it with his 'Character of a fine Gentleman'.

∽

## THE CHARACTER OF A WISE MAN. [*E.B.*]¹

### [By Edmund Burke]

The person I intend to describe is not the wise man of the Stoics, much less is he one of those whom the scripture calls wise unto Salvation; but a mere wise man of this world; one who chooses some desirable end in life and disposes the means of it judiciously and with efficacy. Having given this definition, any further character may seem useless and idle; as to give a Character of prudence and industry in the abstract. But to me it seems otherwise. Those things which appear to depend wholly on reason and prudence have always some inferior supports in our passions; even reason and prudence themselves depend, if not for their substance, yet certainly for their colour and bent on our native constitution and complexions. A certain adjustment of passions, and a certain mode of understanding, are as requisite to form a wise man as a certain degree of reason and good sense.

¹ In ink in a different hand.

A wise man may properly be said to have but two passions, avarice and ambition; the rest are absorbed in these. And if they appear, it is in a subordinate way and to serve the purposes of the two principal.

When he has any end in view, he never looses sight of it; he never suffers it to be sacrificed to intermediate and triffling gratifications. Weak minds cannot fix their eyes steadily on one object. They are soon weary of the pursuit. At the same time that they are unwilling wholly to relinquishing the principal Design, they cannot avoid taking up with some temporary Reliefs, every one of which, however, puts them further and further from their Object.

They waste their whole life without the enjoyment of their pleasures or the establishment of their interest; and drop into their Graves fatigued, restless, anxious, unsatisfied, unsuccessful beings. But the whole life of a wise man is one uniform plot;—everything lends the main design. He knows he cannot enjoy all things, and therefore he drives at some one secure and permanent enjoyment. He leaves nothing to chance; and you might as well take away his Life as make him live extempore. He considers each day only as it does something for the next, and every Year he lives only as it promises a greater interest or grandeur for the future. Yet he is not without the enjoyment of his grandeur or fortune; but this enjoyment only whets him for new ones; and the chief satisfaction he has in them is that they are the certain pledges of more.

He is courageous in an high degree; and knowing that Life without its ends is nothing, he will always venture his life for his ends; and the ends themselves sometimes to extend them. But this never without reason; for his courage is rather of the steady than adventurous kind. He will not move one foot untill he has fixed the other. Yet as he has always a principle of Vigour within him; when he has done so, no frivolous fears shall hinder him from moving both. His pace is not rapid but firm and even. If he does not gain ground as fast as they who move by starts, he never looses any; and is always gaining something. He is called fortunate, and he is so; there happen chances nearly equal to all men; but only those who are ever attentive to their Design, see all the accidents that may tend to it. And it is not that more of these adventures happen to him than to other men; but he knows them when they do happen and knows too how to make use of them. His understanding is strong without being very extensive; and the stronger for being confined. His imagination is neither warm nor bright; so that all his actions are rather to be approved than admired. Vanity is a little passion gratified with little things; and always pernicious to the owner of it. It never gains much, because it lays by nothing, and works always for present pay; it has an appetite early many [*sic*]¹ satisfied but [which] must be fed often. A wise design has been disconcerted because the vain contriver must needs have his wisdom appear as well as his design executed: but the wise man is far above that triffling gratification which puts him in the power of every fool; yet he knows his own value to a scruple; he is even proud to the last degree; a passion which never yet brought any man into contempt but one extremely weak,—a sort of people who are seldom proud. But as he carefully avoids contempt he is not passionate for admiration; he gains a solid esteem attended with solid advantage; he admires no man, esteems very few, and those he esteems he always fears. Those whom he holds in the lowest contempt are good natured men of no great abilities and men of fine parts who are imprudent and unsuccessful in the World. He knows that patient suffering one injury is sure to draw on another; his pride makes him feel all injuries deeply, and his constancy enables him to keep any resolution he has formed. So that his revenge is deep, slow, certain, implaccable and ruinous. On the other hand his friendship is sure; oblige him

¹ Read 'may be'?

and he never forgets it. He understands the Value of a good Office; and that is a great deal. He knows likewise the use of a friend in any design. In choosing his friends he has little regard to the heart or moral character; and once he has chosen a friend, no vice of his can alianate [*sic*] him. He expects them in men. It is not vice but folly he objects to; and as he never much esteems his friends, even something of that he may forgive. But if he should chang[e] his friendship, the object is not neglected but ruined.

In his discourse he is not eloquent, yet he is always very well heard; because no man has ever heard him say a light undigested thing. He seems to say more than he expresses; he has a slowness to determine; he draws all his ideas from experience rather than Speculation; and chooses to appear not so much an agreeable man as a Man of good contrivance and sagacity; and of Action rather than Elocution. He is extremely slow in trusting or believing; and he is confirmed in this disposition every day he lives. When he sees any man perfidious, he grows more cautious. And when he sees another faithful, he does not change his mind; because he believes he has an interest in his fidelity. This belief of men acting more according to their interest than they really do, is what prejudices him more than anything else. He trusts much to himself; this sometimes hurts him too.

He has nothing of that milky quality of good nature which, as it softens, generally something enfeebles the mind. He is in his nature stern, severe, and inflexible. The life of a man is nothing in his eyes if his dying should be anything more conducive to the management of his business than his living. Yet he cannot be said to be cruel or fond of blood, because he never chooses to do anything unnecessary. And he is seldom in the passion of anger.

It is hardness in his Character I take to be the cause why he has no Religion. His passions are not easily moved; and he is incredulous in his nature. He is, besides, proud; apt to reject anything which has a mean aspect in any sense, or is much venerated by mean people. He estimates things merely as they are estimated in the world; and he is always ready to suspect everything of policy and contrivance. In that light he looks upon Religion; which he esteems and despises at once. But he never seeks an empty and foolish reputation from running it down. You cannot discover his Sentiments any otherwise than by his indifference in it and the discoveries which being too cautious of a discovery sometimes makes.

His conversation is not without an agreeable pleasantry; but his mirth is usually dry and sarcastical. His way of loving mankind is but an intercourse of business; not of affection. For he neither loves nor hates anybody. When he marries he makes a good choice because he chooses without passion. Family and fortune he secures; and does not neglect those qualities that may make his Wife an useful and agreeable companion. He makes to her a good husband; but she has not a great deal of his attention; and when she dies, he has a loss of which he is not insensible; but not to that degree which may hinder him of reflecting that his eldest Son may have a better match by the removal of her jointure.

His Children are well educated, and well kept; and in general well instructed to make a figure in the World. Far from being a burden to him, they may be considered as instruments of his Ambition. By advancing them he makes them useful to him; advancing thereby his own importance and grandeur (?)[1] in publick life.

He is steady to his party, and useful to it; and seeks preferment without being servile. In an Office of trust he does not betray it by dishonesty, nor degrade it by inability; but it acquires no dignity under him; and passes to his successor just as he found it. He neglects no usual profit, and scruples no usual

[1] Illegible.

action of whatever nature; but to innovate is dangerous and uncertain; so that, wronging no man in triffles, nor exasperating any by petty injuries; standing no man's rival in inferior accomplishments or pleasures, and serving many for his own ends; ruining those who endeavour to disserve him; being a man to be depended on in business, and adhering to justice whilst it is consistent with sound policy, (and it is not often otherwise), he passes thro affairs with reputation; not being capricious and splenetick; advancing his Children by all means; and not exasperating one set of his neighbours by being of party with the other, he passes for no ill natured Man. Having lived successfully, respected, feared, courted, and something envied; hated but by few, and that secretly; with a Character defended by all the common maxims of Life to which he has always carefully adjusted his conduct, he dies, is emboweld, embalmed, and buried, with a Monument expressing his family, his places, and his Alliances.

## [ 23 ]

This piece might almost have been written at the end rather than at the beginning of Burke's career, so markedly does it seem to mirror his own character and fortunes. It contains, in our opinion, nobility of outlook with a certain sad disillusionment. Cf. my article in *The Times* of 12 January 1938, and see Introduction, p. 10.

### *THE CHARACTER OF A GOOD MAN*

#### [By Edmund Burke]

When a physiologist describes the several complexions of human bodies he considers the melancholic, choleric, phlegmatick and sanguine,—each distinctly by itself, though perhaps they are never found so in nature, and there is hardly any particular man whose complexion does not consist of a mixture of several. There is a similar difference between a General Character and a particular portrait; if, for instance, I am to represent the Character of a stern man without having any individual in my Eye,—every line, every feature of his face ought to Express that disposition; but if I am to draw a picture of some particular man, though that Character is predominant in his countenance, if he has a feature of a turn even directly opposite to it, I ought faithfully to draw it as I find it. The general picture of a Character is in no danger of becoming declamatory or vague by expressing an abstract Quality,—if I represent a wise or a good man, it is still a man I would represent, and everything that belongs to the Human mind is intricate and nice—

What is called good nature is the Basis of the Character of a good man; for nothing else can extend either private friendship or general Beneficence beyond the bounds of mere speculation. This Character is beneficent rather than exactly just; and is not so much distinguished for avoiding carefully everything that is wrong, as for the free Practice of everything that is virtuous; because he is directed in all his actions rather by the impuls[e] of his own excellent spirit than by any exact Rules of Casuistry. If in moral subjects his reasoning is not very Correct, his feelings are fine; all the pictures of his Life are rather great, bold, and unconstrained than Perfectly regular; for which reason they are but little liked by a sort of Precise or citizen-Like minds.

His understanding is fine and subtile; his imagination is lively, active, vigorous, quickly taking fire, and generally too powerful for an understanding fitted rather to conspire with it in its excesses than to restrain it.

This gives its tinct to all his actions; and to every part of his Conversation; which acquire thereby a mellowness, a sweetness, an engaging Quality, which works more on the Affections than on the understanding.

A facility of disposition glares in his Character. Can he, the very Essence of whose soul is to love, to serve, to Oblige everybody in everything,—can he be very exact and nice in weighing and considering when it is proper to comply, and when it is more prudent to Refuse? A mind so rich in benevolence cannot be a great economist of it.

Easy and soft and unsuspicious, it is to be attacked in every Quarter; it is circumvented by fraud, conquer'd by importunity, melted by distress. When it is exerted in its strong side, it is always exerted to be of advantage to others; in its foible, it is fitted so that others may take advantage.

There is nothing in the good man's Character which may make him irreligious, for he has nothing hard, or dry, or proud in his Temper. But his Religion is wholly that of Love; and, to say the truth, it operates less to restrain him when he would go wrong than to inspire and animate him when he pursues his own natural disposition. His devotion is warm and fervent but apt to have intermission. He is not perfect in this point, and he knows that he is not.

There is nothing the good man suspects less in his Constitution than vanity; yet so it is, that he harbours a great deal of that passion, not knowing that he does. He uses no art to Conceal it; therefore it glares in the Eyes of all. Not knowing that he is vain, he takes no settled measures for its gratification; therefore, whilst he seems to do everything for Praise, he gains in reality but very little.

A man of an even Temper, of no violent passions, who never deviates from the Common road of Life, whose desires are not beyond his fortune, nor his affections beyond his family, whose Civilities are his only favours, who with all the power of being actively good is satisfied to be barely harmless, who, with all the ability to be extensively generous, is satisfyed to be commonly honest, whose Ideas of Charity and farthings are inseparably connected; this man is generally well Liked, has a good Character, and not one Enemy in the World. I never knew the good man without many and implacable, because unprovoked, Enemies. For a man that is provoked may be appeased; but what Remedy can you use to cure a man who hates you for your Desire of doing him good?

Envy is very Powerful in all; but it rages more furiously against the little gleams of Prosperity that attend the vertuous than the continual Triumph of Knaves. Against Knaves they may rail; if they are promoted they do not deserve it; and this is a Consolation. But when a good man is advanc'd Envy has no Comfort; it has no subject for railing; and its own heart must own the success was deserved; this is unsupportable and doubles its Effects.

If a bad man chances to fall on some good Action we are surprised; and sometimes begin to suspect that his badness was only seeming—

If a good man falls into an Error we are apt to suspect his goodness was all Hypocrisy.

Is any man to be serv'd or promoted? All turn their eyes on some knave. I am apt to fancy that the fear of such a man, keeping him always in a respectable place in the minds of Men, he is thought of upon every respectable occasion. The Power of Fascination is greater than we sometimes imagine; but the good man, because he is not fear'd, is forgot. No parties are ever form'd in his favour. Whilst he seems himself inattentive to his own Interests, nobody else thinks them worth his attention.

The Life of a good man is a continual satire on mankind; a continual display of their Envy, malignity and ingratitude.

No vicious disposition in the mind stands in need of the sway of reason, and a continual guard, more than this Godlike one of Benevolence. The good man is apt to spend more than he can spare, to borrow more than he can pay, and to Promise more than he can perform; by Which he often appears neither beneficent, just, nor generous.

He serves Chiefly those who want it; and he loves those whom he has serv'd. He is unfortunate by a Consorting with the unfortunate; and he loses all respect himself, because he has other measures of Respect than the World has—

When he is overpowered by Misfortunes where are his friends? Those are his friends who resemble himself; and how many are such? He is no sooner unfortunate than all men see and condemn the imprudence that made him so. Generous minds, that is to say the young and thoughtless, pity and love him; but what avails the Pity of the young and thoughtless? Abandoned by all, he almost becomes a misanthrope. This generous wine is almost soured to vinegar; untill, weary of the world, disappointed in everything here, he seeks other Comforts. He dies transplanted out of a Soil unfriendly to his nature into one where it will be more understood and cultivated. Even [1] the world begins at last to find his Value. The marks of his goodness appear everywhere and are everywhere acknowledged. Even his misfortunes are forgiven, and the selfish themselves begin to discover that they have had a loss.

It may seem that the Marks of Weakness and imprudence which I have given this Character are unsuitable to that only one which we ought to consider as perfect. This I cannot help. I never knew any very good Character without a large Proportion of imprudence. When we hear [a] person call'd a prudent man, Consider what Ideas present themselves first to us, and as it were without seeking? Are not they Ideas of Preserving a man's own person; securing his own Interest, advancing his own Credit? All is self in the picture. It is after some deduction, with a formed design, that we think of applying the Idea of Prudence to the Direction of services done to Another; [2] and when we do, it is always on the defensive and limiting, not on the enlarging, side. The good man, on the Contrary, exerts

[1] A 'yet' or 'but' would seem to be needed before 'even'.
[2] The MS. gives 'Ano<sup>r</sup>'.

his fine understanding rather in making the good more beneficial to the party he would ¹ oblige than in guarding against the ill Consequences of his own Benevolence. It is, besides, worth our Consideration that every passion we have strong enough to make a considerable Principle of Action, is always too strong in some degree for our Reason. The Difference, then, in point of appearing prudent or otherwise is not in the greater or smaller exertion of reason; but in the sort of passion we are disposed to Gratifie. Give a man a selfish passion, like avarice or ambition, it will Certainly pass the boundaries of true Wisdom as much as the most unguarded Benevolence. Yet the Possessors, or rather those possess'd *by* such a passion, whilst they are hurried away by the unbridled Torrent of their passion, seem in general to be guided by the rules of cautious prudence. There is this further to be remark'd.—Selfish passions in reality have mere common reason very much with 'em,—it favours them. But if Reason is exerted by the [*sic*] Benevolence, it is generally on the restraining side, which is its weak side; Especially as it is to resist that Generous Enthusiasm which ever accompanies strong Benevolence.

## [ 24 ]

A piece of very little importance, in which the references are obscure, and of which the authorship is doubtful (see Introduction, p. 9).

⌒

## *VOLTAIRE*

It is impossible to observe upon the faults and Mistakes of Mr Voltaire without observing at the same time upon the Extent of his Capacity and the Spirited Easiness of his Stile

¹ The MS. gives 'woᵈ'.

and manner. Without these advantages, which he possesses in an eminent Degree, it had been impossible to have brought his writings into so general fashion.

A Levity, an inconclusive way of treating difficult points, a decisive tone, and a sententious Manner of saying common things created a Multitude of Admirers and imitators all over Europe. I never remember to have seen in so small a compass as these Extracts contain, so many falsities, Contradictions and absurd Conclusions. It is true any Person who knows this affair[1] only from Mr Voltaire's relation would imagine that this Monument is clear, well authenticated, and existing at this Day. But what will he say when he finds that no such Monument is in being, that its very Existing ever, is mentioned but by one Writer; and that no proof has been given of its Veracity, nor that Ptolemy or any antient Astronomer has made the least use of it.

The valuable Monument, however, which he calls 'without doubt the most valuable Monument of Antiquity', a few paragraphs after becomes a thing of no Consequence at all. 'Of what import' the Union of its 15 k's to a common Logician? The union of the 15 Kingdoms into one prove[s] nothing more than that these Kingdoms were formerly divided and were then united. Or in other words it proves just nothing; but it neither proves that the conquering or conquered States was [*sic*] well peopled or much civilised. Unless we suppose that none but well peopled and civilised Nations make conquests on each other; the very contrary of which is rather true. Does it prove that the tartars were a more civilised and better peopled nation than the Chinese, that they united that Empire to theirs? Does it prove that the Anglo Saxons were an Ancient Nation, well peopled and civilised, because Egbert united their Heptarchy into one Kingdom? Does the great Empire of Attila prove his people numerous and civilised, or that of Tamerlane [and]

[1] It is not clear to what this refers.

119

Gengishsam [*sic*], or do the Conquest[s] of Charlemagne prove his People were more numerous and Civilised than others, unless we suppose that none but the most numerous Nations make great Conquest[s], which is likewise most false. Does this prove that the conquering Country was of more Antiquity than the Conquered[?].

Nor does this Union necessarily require time. He himself proves it does not because one Prince united China and because several Conquerors have united several small States.

Mr Voltaire doubt[s] of nothing himself, and expects his readers should accept of his assertion for Authority;—but— When Historians give us a clearer and more perfect Account of things than could be expected from their means of Information, instead of believing them in those parts, we are apt to suspect they tell us no truth in any points. Thus it is with me when I find Bish. Burnet in the closet of Princes at the age of ten or twelve. With me it brings in doubt the Veracity of what he tells when he might have had a personal knowledge.